Creative Crochet

DARLA SIMS *Creative*

Crochet

Clever Ways to Use Your Yarn Stash

Martingale®
& COMPANY

Creative Crochet: Clever Ways to Use Your Yarn Stash
© 2006 by Darla Sims

Martingale & Company
20205 144th Avenue NE
Woodinville, WA 98072-8478 USA
www.martingale-pub.com

Credits

President .... Nancy J. Martin
CEO .... Daniel J. Martin
COO .... Tom Wierzbicki
Publisher .... Jane Hamada
Editorial Director .... Mary V. Green
Managing Editor .... Tina Cook
Technical Editor .... Donna Druchunas
Copy Editor .... Durby Peterson
Design Director .... Stan Green
Illustrator .... Laurel Strand
Cover and Text Designer .... Stan Green
Studio Photographer .... Brent Kane
Fashion Photographer .... John Hamel
Fashion Stylist .... Pam Simpson
Hair and Makeup Stylist .... Brittany

Printed in China

11 10 09 08 07 06   8 7 6 5 4 3 2 1

Mission Statement

Dedicated to providing quality products and service to inspire creativity.

Library of Congress Cataloging-in-Publication Data

Library of Congress Control Number: 2006020286

ISBN-13: 978-1-56477-687-7

ISBN-10: 1-56477-687-5

Contents

Introduction

Creative Crochet is the result of my own ever-growing yarn stash. The minute you get hooked on any needle art, you become a hoarder, which of course results in what I call "passion stash." Passion stash accumulates faster than it can be used.

For crocheters and knitters, the passion is yarn—furry, fuzzy, fluffy, flat, twisted, shiny, or dull. The three techniques in this book—stripes, ruffles, and cut-and-tie—are based on the art of collage and are bound to open up new, exciting, and unique ways to create our own eye-popping wearables while reducing your yarn stash.

Collage is a technique in which bits and pieces are put together to create a unique work of art. Picasso is often considered the father of collage art, an attribution based on his cubist painting *Still Life with Chair Caning,* created in 1912. However, a number of other futurist artists were incorporating collage elements into their works at the same time. The fun thing about the collage techniques in this book is that they allow the artist residing within you to be freely expressed.

Take a good look at your own stash and you'll surely see that you have accumulated various shades of yarn in your favorite color families—greens, blues, lavenders, reds, or pinks—along with some basic colors such as white, cream, brown, and gray. What to do with such a conglomeration of yarn colors and textures need

no longer elude you. In fact, you're apt to find yourself out shopping once again, seeking out that next perfect color or texture to make the just-right addition to one of the designs that follow or to create an entirely new color family. Once you find yourself hooked on the art of collage crochet, you'll find hunting for yarn as much fun as crocheting these garments and accessories.

Like my own passion stash, the ideas and designs in this book have grown over the years. As a professional designer, I began sorting yarns by color families to make my life simpler. My first sweater design using the cut-and-tie technique was featured in *Cast On* magazine in the 1980s, and I've been building on ways to use collage techniques ever since. This book opens the door to fun crochet techniques and colorful designs.

All the garments and accessories in this book are based on simple, basic stitches and silhouettes. To get even more use out of this book, you can make any of the featured designs in a single color or change the length of a garment or sleeve to get just the look you want.

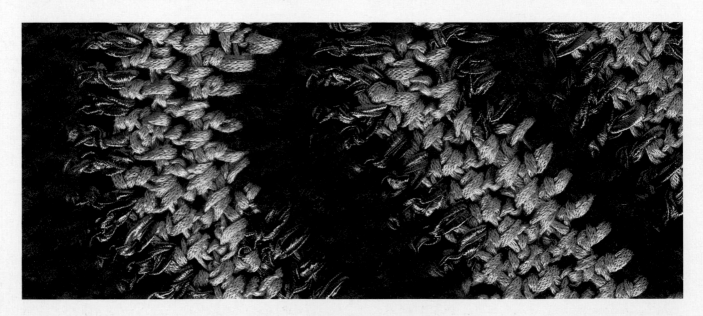

Basics

This chapter includes tips on crocheting sweaters that fit, instructions on caring for handmade sweaters, and an overview of the tools you should have in your crochet bag. You will also find useful information about crochet hook sizes, skill levels, and yarn weights.

The Single Most Important Crochet Factor: Gauge

Even if you don't read any other part of this book, you can't afford to overlook this short section because your gauge (number of stitches and rows per inch) is what determines the final size and fit of any crocheted item. Taking the time to work up a swatch to check your gauge is not just a good idea, it's *critical!*

To make a gauge swatch, crochet a chain approximately 4" long. Then work across the chain in the required stitch or pattern stitch until your swatch is approximately 4" tall. Fasten off. Lay your swatch on a flat surface, smoothing it gently with your hands. Do not touch the swatch again until you have measured.

To determine your gauge, use a stitch gauge tool with an open 2" slot. Count both the stitches and rows within the 2" slot and divide by 2 to determine the number of stitches and rows per inch. Never use a ruler instead of a slotted gauge, because the temptation to smooth out and slightly stretch the fabric to meet a line or measurement on the ruler is more than most people can resist. Smoothing and slightly stretching it almost always results in a distorted and faulty measurement and can dramatically affect the fit of any garment. For example, if the required gauge is 3 stitches per inch and your gauge is really 2½ stitches per inch before you smoothed it out enough to measure 3 stitches per inch, that 2½ stitches per inch is your true gauge.

For most of the garments in this book, the required gauge is 3 stitches per inch. So if the pattern requires 60 stitches across, the sweater will be 20" wide (3 stitches per inch times 20" equals 60 stitches). If you have distorted your swatch by smoothing and your true gauge is only 2½ stitches per inch, then the actual width of your 60 stitches will be 24", which is 4" wider than required. If your back and front are each 4" wider than required, the end result is a sweater that is 8" too large around the bust. Taking the time to work up a preliminary swatch actually saves time overall and eliminates guesswork. If your gauge is accurate, your finished garment will fit properly.

The hook sizes given in any pattern are only guidelines, but the gauge given is a *must* for a perfect fit. In other words, consider the required gauge "written in stone." If you find you have too few stitches per inch and your swatch is too big, try again with a smaller hook; likewise, if you have too many stitches per inch and your swatch is too small, try a larger hook.

Do not begin a project until your number of stitches per inch is correct. The number of rows per inch is not as vital, because you can add or subtract rows to get the length you want. But if you want a sweater to fit around the bust, your number of stitches per inch must be correct beginning with the first row.

Ease, Fit, and Sizing

Ease is the number of inches around the bustline of garment compared to an actual bust measurement. Fit and ease are personal preferences, and they are important factors to consider before deciding which pattern size fits your needs the best.

Many people know how they like a garment to fit or feel when worn, but have no idea how much actual ease they prefer. To find out your own preferred ease, head to your closet or dresser drawers and pull out a garment with a silhouette that is similar to the one you plan to crochet. Do not choose a garment of woven fabric; instead, choose a sweater or cotton knit that has some natural give. Lay that garment on a flat surface and use a tape measure to measure from side to side across the front, just beneath armholes. Most people are surprised by this measurement and quickly understand why their handmade sweaters don't fit as expected.

If you like a snug fit, a 2" ease may be just right. The majority of people prefer an ease of 3" to 4", while others like a more generous ease for a looser fit. Knowing the amount of ease you prefer gives you a measurement to use as a guideline in determining which pattern size suits you.

Laundering Garments Crocheted with Varied Fibers

When using yarns of the same fiber content, follow the yarn label instructions for laundering crocheted sweaters. Crocheted sweaters created by using stripes, ruffles, or the cut-and-tie technique contain yarns with a wide variety of fibers, yet I'm still using the same best method for laundering these priceless garments that I have used from the beginning: Using a mild soap or shampoo and tepid water, let the sweater soak in soapy water for five to ten minutes; then gently squeeze the suds through the entire sweater. Gently squeeze out (do not wring) excess suds from the sweater and rinse it thoroughly in tepid water. Roll the sweater in a fluffy towel and repeat with a second towel, allowing the sweater to sit at least five minutes so the towel can absorb as much moisture as possible. Gently unroll the sweater and lay it out flat to dry, smoothing the garment gently into shape.

Regardless of the differences in the fibers and yarns I have used for more than 25 years, this method has always produced wonderful results.

Essential Tools

Stitch Gauge Tool. Other than a crochet hook, a stitch gauge tool is the single most important tool for a crocheter and is an absolute must! Remember that your gauge is the number of stitches and rows per a specific measurement. This gauge determines the ultimate measurements and fit of any garment. A stitch gauge tool with an open slot helps isolate stitches and rows in the most precise way. (See page 7 for instructions on measuring gauge.)

Scale. Use this to weigh opened skeins.

Tape Measure. You will need this for measuring your piece after smoothing it on a flat surface.

Pincushion. This keeps your pins and various sizes of needles, for both yarn and hand sewing, all in one place.

Color-Ended Ball-Point Pins. Using ball-point pins instead of standard pins helps avoid split or snagged yarn.

Scissors. I prefer small, titanium scissors for the sharpest, cleanest cut.

Plastic Locking Stitch Markers. Never use safety pins in place of plastic markers, because yarn can easily become caught and tangled in the coils of safety pins. Use plastic locking stitch markers to mark color changes, increases and decreases, panels, isolated stitches or stitch patterns, and to track stitch and row count.

Decorative Box. Keep all your tools tucked neatly away and out of sight in a pretty little box similar to the one shown in the photo. If you make a habit of always putting your tools away in your box, you'll never waste time looking for a tool again.

Tapestry Needle. You will use this for weaving in ends and sewing seams.

Crochet Hooks. The millimeter size is the most accurate for selecting hooks; the letter or number given for the U.S. size may vary from manufacturer to manufacturer.

CROCHET HOOK SIZES

Millimeter Range	U.S. Size Range*
2.25 mm	B-1
2.75 mm	C-2
3.25 mm	D-3
3.5 mm	E-4
3.75 mm	F-5
4 mm	G-6
4.5 mm	7
5 mm	H-8
5.5 mm	I-9
6 mm	J-10
6.5 mm	K-10½
8 mm	L-11
9 mm	M/N-13
10 mm	N/P-15

*Letter or number may vary. Rely on the millimeter sizing.

SKILL LEVELS

■□□□ **Beginner:** Projects for first-time crocheters using basic stitches. Minimal shaping.

■■□□ **Easy:** Projects using yarn with basic stitches, repetitive stitch patterns, simple color changes, and simple shaping and finishing.

■■■□ **Intermediate:** Projects using a variety of techniques, such as basic lace patterns or color patterns, and midlevel shaping and finishing.

YARN WEIGHTS

Yarn-Weight Symbol and Category Names	1 SUPER FINE	2 FINE	3 LIGHT	4 MEDIUM	5 BULKY	6 SUPER BULKY
Types of Yarns in Category	Sock, Fingering, Baby	Sport, Baby	DK, Light Worsted	Worsted, Afghan, Aran	Chunky, Craft, Rug	Bulky, Roving
Crochet Gauge Ranges in Single Crochet to 4"	21 to 32 sts	16 to 20 sts	12 to 17 sts	11 to 14 sts	8 to 11 sts	5 to 9 sts
Recommended Hook in Metric Size Range	2.25 to 3.5 mm	3.5 to 4.5 mm	4.5 to 5.5 mm	5.5 to 6.5 mm	6.5 to 9 mm	9 mm and larger
Recommended Hook in U.S. Size Range	B-1 to E-4	E-4 to E-7	7 to I-9	I-9 to K-10½	K-10½ to M-13	M-13 and larger

Let's Crochet

This section covers the basic crochet stitches you'll need to get started with the projects, as well as a list of crochet abbreviations. Single crochet, half double crochet, double crochet, treble crochet, and slip stitch are the five basic crochet stitches. If you have questions, read this to familiarize yourself with the basics. If you're more experienced, check back here when you need a reminder about a specific technique.

Making a Chain

1. Make a slipknot and place it on the hook.
2. Holding the crochet hook in your right hand and the yarn in your left hand, bring the yarn over the hook from front to back, turning the hook slightly to keep the yarn on the hook. Draw the yarn through the slipknot.

   Repeat step 2 until the chain has the required number of stitches.

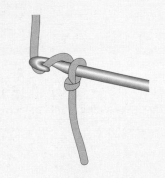

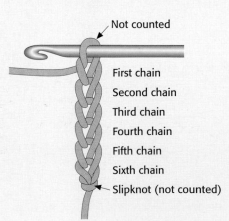

Not counted

First chain
Second chain
Third chain
Fourth chain
Fifth chain
Sixth chain
Slipknot (not counted)

Single Crochet

Row 1

1. Chain 11 loosely.
2. Insert the hook into the top loop of the second chain from the hook.

3. Bring the yarn over your hook as before (this is called "yarn over" in most published instructions), and draw the yarn through the loop made in step 2—two loops on the hook.
4. Yarn over again, and pull the yarn through both loops on the hook; first single crochet made.

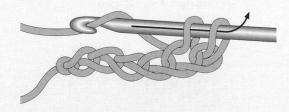

5. Insert the hook into the next chain and pull up a loop—two loops on the hook.
6. Yarn over and pull the yarn through both loops on the hook; a single crochet made.

Repeat steps 5 and 6 along the entire chain to complete the row.

Row 2

1. To begin the next row, you must make a turning chain to bring the yarn to the height of the first stitch of the next row. Make one chain.

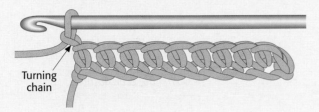

Turning chain

2. Turn work around.

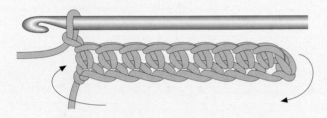

3. Insert the hook under both top loops of the first single crochet (closest to the hook), yarn over, and draw a loop through.

First single crochet in row

4. Yarn over again and draw the yarn through both loops on the hook; single crochet made.

Repeat in each stitch to the end of the row. You should have 10 single crochet stitches.

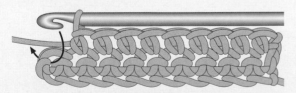

Last single crochet in row

Fasten Off

At the end of the last row of your work, cut the yarn, leaving a 4" to 6" tail. Pull the tail through the last loop on the hook and pull to tighten.

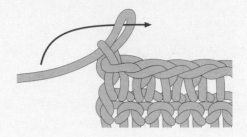

Half Double Crochet

Row 1

1. Chain 11 loosely.
2. Yarn over, insert the hook in the third chain from the hook, yarn over again and pull up a loop—three loops on the hook.

3. Yarn over and pull the yarn through all three loops on the hook; first half double crochet made.

4. Yarn over, insert the hook in the next chain and pull up a loop—three loops on the hook.
5. Yarn over and draw the yarn through all three loops on the hook; half double crochet made.

Repeat steps 4 and 5 along the entire chain to complete the row.

Row 2

To begin the next row, you must make a turning chain. Make two chains to reach the height of a half double crochet stitch. Skip the first stitch, and half double crochet in each double crochet stitch across the row, working the last half double crochet stitch in the top of the turning chain from the previous row. You should have 9 half double crochet stitches plus the beginning chain for a total of 10 stitches.

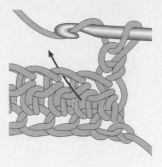

Double Crochet

Row 1

1. Chain 12 loosely.
2. Yarn over, keeping the yarn on the hook, insert the hook into the fourth chain from the hook, and pull up a loop—three loops on hook.

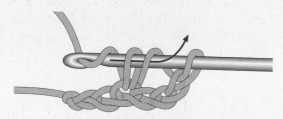

3. Yarn over and draw the yarn through the first two loops—two loops remain on the hook.

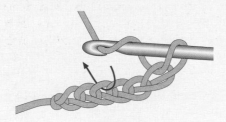

4. Yarn over and draw the yarn through the remaining two loops; first double crochet made.

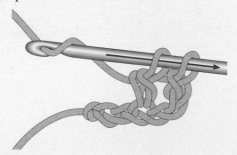

5. Yarn over, insert the hook in the next chain, yarn over and pull up the loop—three loops on the hook.
6. Yarn over, draw the yarn through the first two loops on the hook.
7. Yarn over and draw the yarn through the remaining two loops on the hook; double crochet made.

Repeat steps 5–7 along the entire chain to complete the row.

Row 2

Chain three stitches (turning chain); these three chains count as the first double crochet of the row. Skip the first stitch, and double crochet in each double crochet stitch across the row, working the last double crochet stitch in the top of the beginning chain three. Double crochet inserting the hook under both top loops of the next double crochet from the previous row. You should have 9 double crochet stitches plus the beginning chain for a total of 10 stitches.

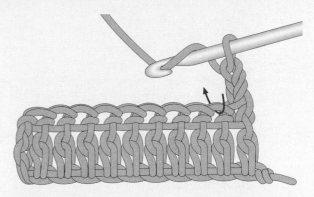

Treble Crochet

This stitch is also called triple crochet.

Row 1

1. Chain 13 loosely.
2. Yarn over twice, insert the hook in the fifth chain from the hook, yarn over and pull up a loop—four loops on the hook.

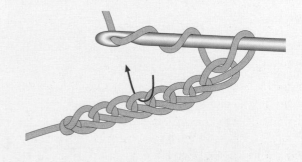

3. Yarn over and draw the yarn through the first two loops on the hook—three loops remain on the hook.

4. Yarn over and draw the yarn through the next two loops on the hook—two loops remain on the hook.

5. Yarn over and draw the yarn through the remaining two loops on the hook; treble crochet made.

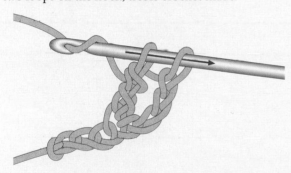

6. Yarn over twice, insert the hook in the next chain, yarn over and pull up a loop—four loops on the hook.
7. Yarn over and draw the yarn through the first two loops on the hook.
8. Yarn over and draw the yarn through the next two loops on the hook.
9. Yarn over and draw the yarn through the remaining two loops on the hook; treble crochet made.

Repeat steps 5–9 along the entire chain to complete the row.

Row 2

Chain four stitches (this counts as the first treble crochet of the row), turn work. Skip the first stitch, treble crochet in the next treble crochet stitch and in each stitch across the row, working the last treble crochet in the top of the turning chain. You should have 9 treble crochet stitches plus the beginning chain for a total of 10 stitches.

Slip Stitch

Slip stitch is used to join work or to move yarn across work to shape the fabric without adding height to it.

1. Chain 12. Turn work without making a turning chain.
2. Insert the hook in the first stitch, yarn over and draw the yarn through both the stitch and the loop on the hook; slip stitch made.

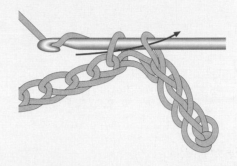

Turning Chains

The number of chains required for turning a row is based on the height of a stitch. The following illustration shows the height of various stitches. To turn rows, chain:

0 for slip stitch

1 for single crochet

2 for half double crochet

3 for double crochet

4 for treble crochet

Note: The turning chain at the end of each row counts as the first stitch of the next row for half double, double, and treble crochet. The turning chain does *not* count as a stitch for single crochet.

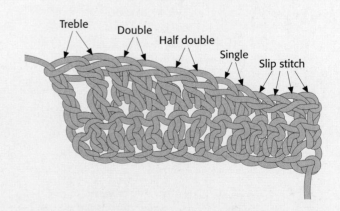

Front-Post Single Crochet (FPsc)

Insert the hook from the front to the back around the indicated stitch, yarn over, and pull up the loop even with the last stitch worked, yarn over, and pull through both the loops on the hook.

Front-Post Double Crochet (FPdc)

Yarn over, insert the hook from the front to the back around the post of the stitch indicated, yarn over, and pull up a loop even with the stitch on the hook, (yarn over and draw through two loops on the hook) twice.

Increasing

Increasing is commonly used to shape garments. For example, a sleeve begins at the wrist and increases in width to the top of the sleeve, requiring increases to be made along the way. When you are working in a pattern stitch, instructions are usually provided for increases that are specific to that pattern stitch.

When crocheting with single crochet, half double crochet, double crochet, or treble crochet, the most common way of increasing is to work two or more stitches in the same stitch.

Decreasing

Decreasing is used to make a crochet piece narrower, for example, when you are shaping an armhole or a neckline.

Decreasing is usually accomplished by working two stitches together, which then count as one stitch. Whether you are working in single crochet, half double crochet, or double crochet, work the first stitch without completing the final step, work the second stitch in the same manner, yarn over and draw the yarn through all loops on the hook; decrease made. These steps are abbreviated sc2tog, hdc2tog, and dc2tog.

You can also work three stitches together in the same manner to decrease two stitches at once. These steps are abbreviated sc3tog, hdc3tog, and dc3tog.

Beginning Decreases

The following decreases are used at the beginning of a new row. They are less bulky than standard decreases.

Beginning Single Crochet Decrease (beg sc dec)

At the end of the previous row, chain one, and turn work. Insert the hook in the first stitch and draw the yarn through, insert hook in next stitch, and then yarn over and draw the yarn through all three loops on the hook.

Beginning Half Double Crochet Decrease (beg hdc dec)

At the end of the previous row, chain one only, and turn work. Yarn over, insert the hook in the first stitch of the row, draw the yarn through, yarn over and draw the yarn through all four loops on the hook.

Beginning Double Crochet Decrease (beg dc dec)

At the end of the previous row, chain two only, and turn. Work yarn over, insert the hook in the second stitch of the row, draw the yarn through two loops; yarn over, insert the hook into the next stitch, draw the yarn through two loops; decrease made.

CROCHET ABBREVIATIONS

( ) Work instructions within parentheses as many times as directed.

* * Repeat instructions between asterisks as many times as directed or repeat from a given set of instructions

beg	begin(ning)	oz	ounce(s)
bl	back loop(s)	patt	pattern(s)
ch	chain or chain stitch(es)	rem	remain(ing)
cont	continue(ing)	rep(s)	repeat(s)
dc	double crochet(s)	rnd	round(s)
dc2tog	double crochet 2 stitches together (decrease)	RS	right side
		sc	single crochet(s)
dc3tog	double crochet 3 stitches together (double decrease)	sc2tog	single crochet 2 stitches together (decrease)
dec	decrease(ing)(s)	sc3tog	single crochet 3 stitches together (double decrease)
dtr	double treble(s)		
fl	front loop(s)	sk	skip
FPdc	front-post double crochet	sl st	slip stitch
FPsc	front-post single crochet	sp(s)	space(s)
g	gram(s)	st(s)	stitch(es)
hdc	half double crochet(s)	tch	turning chain(s)
hdc2tog	half double crochet 2 stitches together (decrease)	tog	together
		tr	treble crochet(s)
hdc3tog	half double crochet 3 stitches together (double decrease)	WS	wrong side
		yd(s)	yard(s)
inc	increase(ing)(s)	YO	yarn over
m	meter(s)		

Special Techniques

As mentioned on page 6, I've developed three special techniques for using up leftover yarn from a crocheter's stash: working in stripes, crocheting ruffles, and using the cut-and-tie method. I explain each of these techniques in this section.

Because the projects in this book all use leftover yarns, and because you can combine yarns of different weights and fibers, I have listed the required yarn amount for each project in ounces rather than yards. You can easily weigh a bunch of open skeins to determine the total weight, but determining the total yardage would be almost impossible.

Metric Conversions

For unopened skeins, use these handy formulas to easily convert yards to meters and ounces to grams or vice versa so you can calculate how much yarn you'll need for your project.

m	=	yd	x	0.9144
yds	=	m	x	1.0936
g	=	oz	x	28.3500
oz	=	g	x	0.0352

Changing Colors

All my special techniques use multiple colors. Whether you change colors at the end or somewhere within a row, the rule remains the same: always pull the new color through the last loop worked with the old color, and then cut and tie off the old color securely unless instructed otherwise.

Stripe Techniques

Crocheting in stripes needs little if any explanation. You simply change colors at the ends of rows. Stripes can be varied by increasing or decreasing the number of rows per stripe as you like.

Ruffle Techniques

Designs using the ruffle technique are really based on stripes too—they just look different. Some of the romantic designs appear to be filled with ruffles, but they are simply stripes of shells. Generally, shells are created by skipping a given number of stitches, working that same number of stitches into one specified stitch, and then skipping the same number of stitches again. For example, skip three, work three into one stitch, and skip three again. This technique allows the shell to fan out over the skipped stitches. All ruffles are fun and interesting to crochet.

Cut-and-Tie Techniques

There are two ways to cut and tie. The first method is fairly simple: simply cut lengths of yarn that vary from 1 foot to 2 yards in length. Cut and tie the lengths together, rolling the yarn into a ball every few yards.

I prefer the second method because it gives me more control over the placement of various shades and textures as I crochet the fabric. Make a chain in the same yarn that you plan to use for trim or edging. As you work across the first row, change color once (you now have two colors in the first row). Make this first change in color after working across approximately one-third of the row. When working across the second row, add a third color between the other two colors. To do so, work three or four fewer stitches than the previous row for the first color, tie in the new color, and work to within three or four stitches of the last color. This movement of a few stitches per row will create diagonal lines in your color work.

Before starting the third row, select another hue of your color family that looks good with the three colors already used. Decide where you wish to add the color, cutting one previous color when you reach that point. Continue to move colors to create slanted instead of straight lines. You can change colors on either the right or wrong side of your work, but be sure to carry the tails on the wrong side and work over them to decrease the finishing work.

To create the most attractive results, it helps to think of the changes of texture and color as little blocks that have slanted ends, because this will create blocks that are more visually appealing than square blocks. You can change colors where and when you please. I seldom work more than five or six rows of any single shade of a color family; however, you may work larger, deeper sections of color. Work colors in the way that you prefer.

Although the majority of yarns for all the sweaters made using the cut-and-tie technique are medium-weight, you can use a small amount of bulky-weight yarns for added texture or color. When doing so, maintain gauge by working all bulky weights using a hook that is one size smaller than the size used previously. To avoid distorting gauge, limit the use of bulky weights to no more than 10% of the total yarn. In general, incorporating bulky-weight yarns works best when you crochet only a limited number of stitches, for example, when you crochet 15 stitches and only one row in a bulky weight. It takes only a few stitches to make a visual impact. Remember to change your hook size when resuming work with medium-weight yarn!

Once you've worked with each of the yarns selected, you may wonder how to continue. At this point, it's sometimes helpful to work a single row in one color, making a break in any sequence of shape or shade, and then to start color placement once again. To keep a random look, avoid duplicating color placements you have already used. Taking another look at the photo of the sweater you're crocheting will also help you make decisions about color changes. Before you know it, you'll develop a rhythm and sense of when and where to make color changes.

Because all the cut-and-tie sweaters in this book are based on half double or double crochet, there are no fancy stitch patterns to learn. You can concentrate on shades and textures of yarn instead of on changing stitches as you work. When working with fuzzy or highly textured yarns that make stitches difficult to see, be sure to count your stitches per row to ensure that you don't lose a stitch along the way.

As your fabric grows, so will your enthusiasm. When you must put your work down, you'll find yourself thinking about it and forming ideas for what to do when you next begin to work. It's fascinating and exciting to see what is happening to all those colors and textures. Best of all, you can apply these cut-and-tie techniques to other sweater patterns and turn them into works of art as well. I hope you will find this technique as stimulating and fun as I do!

All the cut-and-tie designs on pages 52–79 provide basic instructions—you are the artist! Simply use the suggestions given here to create your own one-of-a-kind garment.

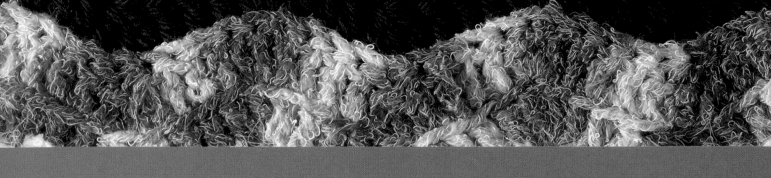

Striped Projects

White-on-White Short-Sleeved Cardigan

Just right to wear on its own, this little jacket also makes a great cover-up for a camisole or other top.

Skill Level

Easy

■■□□

Size

Small (Medium, Large, Extra Large)

Finished Measurements

Bust: 36 (40, 44, 48)"

Length: 22½ (23, 23½, 24)"

Materials

- Approx 12 (14, 16, 18) oz *total* of medium-weight and bulky-weight yarns in 17 assorted whites or the colors of your choice ④ ⑤
- Size G-6 (4 mm) crochet hook or size required to obtain gauge
- Size H-8 (5 mm) crochet hook or size required to obtain gauge
- 434 (464, 504, 664) pearl beads, 6 mm diameter
- 9 pearl buttons, ⅜" diameter
- Sewing needle and thread
- Tapestry needle for sewing seams and weaving in ends

Gauge

6 hdc and 5 rows = 2" using larger hook and medium-weight yarn and using smaller hook and bulky-weight yarn

Lower Body

Note: The lower body is worked in one piece from side to side. Change colors as desired. Two rows create one stripe.

With large hook and medium-weight yarn, ch 43.

Row 1 (RS): Hdc in 3rd ch from hook, hdc in each rem ch, turn—42 hdc.

Row 2: Ch 2 (counts as 1 hdc, now and throughout), hdc in 2nd hdc and in each hdc to end. Change yarn, turn.

Row 3: Ch 2, hdc to end, turn.

Work even in hdc until 45 (50, 55, 60) stripes have been completed, which will be 90 (100, 110, 120) rows. End with WS row. Fasten off.

Upper Body

Note: The same yarn was used for both fronts; a different yarn was used for the back. The fronts are decorated with beads.

Foundation Row (WS): Turn body sideways, working over end sts of each row, attach yarn to first st, ch1, 1 sc in same st, *2 sc in next st, 4 sc; rep from * to last 4 sts, ending 2 sc in next st, 3 sc, turn—108 (120, 132, 144) sc.

Shape Right-Front Armhole and V-neck

Row 1 (RS): Ch1, beg hdc dec, 1 hdc in each of next 25 (28, 31, 34) sts—26 (29, 32, 35) sts total in right front. Cut yarn, thread 26 (29, 32, 35) pearl beads onto yarn, reattach yarn and turn.

Row 2: Ch 2, YO, insert hook in 2nd st and pull yarn through, slip pearl bead close to hook on WS of work, YO and pull yarn through all 3 loops on hook. *YO, insert hook in next st and pull yarn through, slip bead up to hook on WS, YO and pull yarn through all 3 loops on hook; rep from * to end, turn.

Work rows 1 and 2 another 2 times; 3 pearl stripes completed—24 (27, 30, 33) sts rem.

Cont to dec 1 st at neck edge every other row until 18 sts (20, 22, 24) sts rem.

Work even until armhole depth measures 8½ (9, 9½, 10)". Fasten off.

Shape Left-Front Armhole and V-neck

Row 1 (RS): Sk 54 (60, 66, 72) sts for back, attach yarn to next st, ch 2, hdc in each st to last 2 sts, hdc2tog, turn—26 (29, 32, 35) sts total in left front. Cut yarn, thread 26 (29, 32, 35) pearl beads onto yarn, reattach yarn.

Row 2: Ch 2, hdc across, working beads as for right front, turn.

Work rows 1 and 2 another 2 times; 3 pearl stripes completed—24 (27, 30, 33) sts rem.

Cont to dec 1 st at neck edge only, every other row until 18 (20, 22, 24) sts rem.

Work even until same length as right front. Fasten off.

Upper Back

Row 1: Attach yarn to first skipped st, ch 2, hdc in each of next 53 (59, 65, 71) sts, turn—54 (60, 66, 72) sts.

Row 2: Ch 2, hdc across, turn.

Rep row 2 until back is same length as fronts. Fasten off.

Finishing

With RS tog, sew shoulder seams.

Armhole Edging

Rnd 1 (RS): Using smaller hook and medium-weight yarn, beg at shoulder seam and work 50 (52, 54, 56) sc around armhole; join. Do not turn.

Rnd 2 (RS): Ch1, 1 sc in same st as joining, sc around; join and turn. Cut yarn, thread on 50 (54, 54, 56) pearl beads, and reattach yarn.

Rnd 3 (WS): Ch 1, 1 sc in same st as joining, work in pearl beads as for yoke; join and turn.

Rnd 4 (RS): Ch 1, sc around. Join and fasten off.

Outer Edging

Rnd 1 (RS): Beg at lower corner of left front, working across bottom of jacket, working over end sts of hdc rows, *1 sc in each of next 4 sts, 2 sc in next st; rep from * to corner, 3 sc in corner, 1 sc in each st along front to V-neck shaping, work 3 sc in st where V-neck shaping begins, 30 (32, 34, 36) sc to shoulder seam, 17 (19, 21, 23) sc across back neck, 30 (32, 34, 36) sc from shoulder seam to V-neck shaping, work 3 sc in st where V-neck shaping begins, 42 sc to beg corner; join. Place markers for 9 evenly spaced buttons on left front, turn.

Rnd 2: Ch 1, sc to first marker, (ch 3, sl st in last st made to make buttonhole) 9 times, sc in each st around, working 3 sc in each corner. Join and fasten off.

Sew on buttons.

Designer Tip

Use glass, wooden, or metal beads instead of pearl beads to complement yarns in your stash for your own unique look.

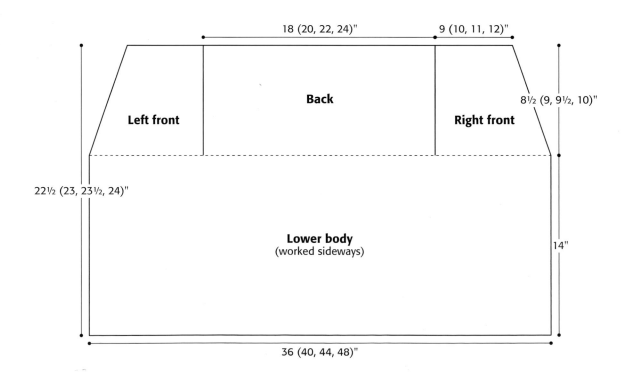

18 (20, 22, 24)" 9 (10, 11, 12)"

Back

Left front

Right front

8½ (9, 9½, 10)"

22½ (23, 23½, 24)"

Lower body
(worked sideways)

14"

36 (40, 44, 48)"

Versatile Vest

At the end of the work-day, remove your suit jacket and you're ready for an evening out. This is a good project for those little odds and ends we all seem to have in our stash.

Skill Level
Easy

Size
Small (Medium, Large, Extra Large)

Finished Measurements
Bust: 38 (42, 46, 50)"
Length: 18½ (19, 19½, 20)"

Materials

- Approx 10 (12, 14, 16) oz *total* of 9 different medium-weight and bulky-weight yarns in the colors of your choice
- Size G-6 (4 mm) crochet hook or size required to obtain gauge
- Size H-8 (5 mm) crochet hook or size required to obtain gauge
- Tapestry needle for sewing seams and weaving in ends

Gauge

6 sts and 7 rows = 2" with larger hook and medium-weight yarn and with smaller hook and bulky-weight yarn

Back

Note: Using colors at random, make stripes of varying widths by crocheting one to five rows per color. If you prefer a more structured look, change colors every two, three, or four rows. Give yourself the freedom to make this top any way you like.

Using larger hook and medium-weight yarn, ch 59 (65, 71, 77).

Row 1 (RS): Hdc in third ch from hook and in each ch to end—58 (64, 70, 76) hdc, turn.

Row 2: Ch 2 (counts as first hdc now and throughout), hdc to end.

Rep row 2, changing colors as you like. Work even in hdc until piece measures 10" or desired length to underarm, ending with a WS row. Fasten off.

Note: If you wish to make the length longer than 10", you will need more yarn.

Shape Armhole

Row 1 (RS): Sk first 5 (6, 7, 8) hdc, attach yarn to next hdc and ch 2, hdc to last 5 (6, 7, 8) sts, leaving them unworked for armhole, turn—48 (52, 56, 60) hdc sts.

Row 2: Ch 1, beg hdc dec, hdc to last 2 sts, hdc2tog, turn—46 (50, 54, 58) hdc sts.

Row 3: Ch 2, hdc to end, turn.

Work rows 2 and 3 another 3 times—40 (44, 48, 52) hdc rem. Work even in hdc until back measures 18½ (19, 19½, 20)". Fasten off.

Front

Work as for back to armhole shaping.

Left Armhole and Neck

Row 1 (RS): Sk first 5 (6, 7, 8) hdc, attach yarn to next hdc and ch 1, work beg hdc dec over first 2 sts, 1 hdc in each of next 20 (22, 24, 26) sts, 2 hdc tog, leave rem sts unworked, turn—22 (24, 26, 28) hdc.

Row 2: Ch 2, hdc to end, turn.

Cont to dec 1 st at armhole edge every RS row another 3 times, while AT SAME TIME, cont to dec 1 st at neck edge every RS row another 9 (10, 11, 12) times—10 (11, 12, 13) hdc rem for shoulder.

Work even in hdc until armhole depth measures 8½ (9, 9½, 10)". Fasten off.

Right Armhole and Neck

Row 1 (RS): Beg in center st next to left front, attach yarn, ch 1, beg hdc dec over first 2 sts, 1 hdc in each of next 20 (22, 24, 26) sts, hdc2tog; leave last 5 (6, 7, 8) sts unworked—22 (24, 26, 28) hdc, turn.

Row 2: Ch 2, hdc to end.

Cont to dec 1 st at armhole edge every RS row another 3 times, while AT SAME TIME, cont to dec 1 st at neck edge every RS row another 9 (10, 11, 12) times—10 (11, 12, 13) hdc rem for shoulder.

Work even in hdc until armhole depth measures 8½ (9, 9½, 10)". Fasten off.

Finishing

With RS tog, sew shoulder and side seams.

Neck Edging

Rnd 1: With RS facing you and using smaller hook and color of choice, work 1 rnd in sc around neck, working sc3tog at lower V. Join.

Rnd 2: Work 1 rnd of sc using contrasting yarn. Join and fasten off.

Lower-Body Edging

With RS facing you and using smaller hook and color of choice, beg at side seam, work 1 rnd evenly spaced sc around lower edge of body. Join and fasten off.

Armhole Edging

With RS facing you and using smaller hook and color of choice, beg at underarm seam, work 1 rnd evenly spaced sc around armhole. Join and fasten off.

Rep on 2nd armhole.

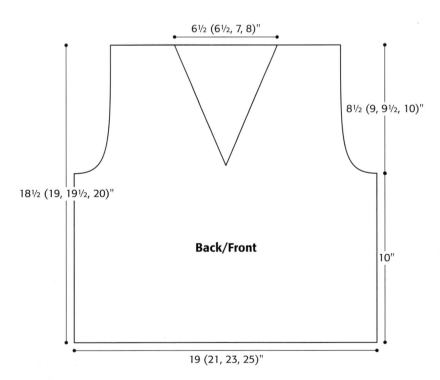

6½ (6½, 7, 8)"

8½ (9, 9½, 10)"

18½ (19, 19½, 20)"

Back/Front

10"

19 (21, 23, 25)"

Waves-of-Blue Striped Pullover

Increase a few stitches here, decrease a few stitches there, and a stripe becomes a wave. This versatile sweater is the solution when you have substituted yarn in an afghan or sweater and miscalculated the amount. Use two or three skeins of a single color as the main color, and mix with assorted smaller amounts of the same color family.

Skill Level

Easy

Size

Small (Medium, Large, Extra Large)

Finished Measurements

Bust: 36 (42, 48, 54)"

Length: 24 (24½, 25, 25½)"

Materials

- Approx 42 (46, 50, 54) oz *total* of medium-weight and bulky-weight yarns in 15 shades of blue or the colors of your choice. Of this total amount, you will need approx 8 (10, 12, 14) oz in MC for sleeves and neck edging. 〔4〕 〔5〕
- Size G-6 (4 mm) crochet hook or size required to obtain gauge
- Size H-8 (5 mm) crochet hook or size required to obtain gauge
- Tapestry needle for sewing seams and weaving in ends

Gauge

1 wave patt and 4 rows = 3" using larger hook and medium-weight yarn and using smaller hook and bulky-weight yarn for body

6 dc and 5 rows = 2" using larger hook and medium-weight yarn for sleeves

Back

Note: Change colors as directed. Two rows create one stripe.

With larger hook and medium-weight yarn, ch 63 (73, 83, 93).

Row 1 (RS): Dc in 3rd ch from hook, *1 dc in each of next 3 ch (YO, insert hook in next ch, YO and pull through 2 loops) 3 times, YO and pull through all 4 loops on hook; dc3tog made, 1 dc in each of next 3 ch, 3 dc in next ch; rep from * to last 4 ch, 1 dc in each of next 3 ch, 2 dc in last ch, turn—6 (7, 8, 9) waves.

Row 2: Ch 3 (counts as 1 dc now and throughout), 1 dc in first st, * working in fl across, 1 dc in each of next 3 sts, dc3tog, 3 dc, 3 dc in next st; rep from * to last 4 sts, 1 dc in each of next 3 ch, 2 dc in top of tch. Change color, turn.

Row 3: Ch 3, 1 dc in first st, * working in bl across, 1 dc in each of next 3 sts, dc3tog, 3 dc, 3 dc in next st; rep from * to last 4 sts, 1 dc in each of next 3 ch, 2 dc in top of tch, turn.

Rep rows 2 and 3, changing colors every 2 rows until 16 (16, 18, 18) stripes are complete. Fasten off.

Front

Work as for back until 14 (14, 16, 16) stripes are complete.

Shape Left Neck

Sizes Small and Medium only:

Row 1 (RS): Ch 3 (counts as 1 dc now and throughout), 1 dc in first st, (working in bl across, 1 dc in each of next 3 sts, dc3tog, 3 dc, 3 dc in next st) twice, 1 dc in each of next 3 ch, 2 dc in top of next st, turn.

Rows 2–4: Work across in established wave patt. Fasten off.

Size Large only:

Rows 1 and 3 (RS): Ch 3 (counts as 1 dc now and throughout), 1 dc in first st, (working in bl across, 1 dc in each of next 3 sts, 3 dc tog, 3 dc, 3 dc in next st) twice, 1 dc in each of next 3 ch, 2 dc in top of next st, 3 dc, dc3tog, turn.

Rows 2 and 4: Ch 3, 1 dc in each of next 4 sts, 3 dc in next st, complete row in patt. Fasten off.

Size Extra Large only:

Row 1 (RS): Ch 3 (counts as 1 dc now and throughout), 1 dc in first st, (working in bl across, 1 dc in each of next 3 sts, dc3tog, 3 dc, 3 dc in next st) 3 times, 1 dc in each of next 3 ch, 2 dc in top of next st, turn.

Rows 2–4: Work across in established wave patt. Fasten off.

Shape Right Neck

Sizes Small and Medium only:

Row 1 (RS): Attach yarn to st that corresponds to last st of row 1 of left neck, skipping center sts for neck, and work to end in patt, turn.

Rows 2–4: Ch 3, work in established wave patt. Fasten off.

Size Large only:

Row 1 (RS): Attach yarn to dc3tog that corresponds to last st of row 1 of left neck, ch 3, work to end in patt, turn.

Row 2: Ch 3, work in patt to last 3 sts, dc3tog, turn.

Row 3: Ch 2, (YO, insert hook in next st and pull yarn through 2 loops) twice (counts as dc3tog), complete row in wave patt, turn.

Row 4: Ch 3, work in patt to last 3 sts, dc3tog. Fasten off.

Size Extra Large only:

Row 1 (RS): Attach yarn to st that corresponds to last st of row 1 of left neck, skipping center sts omitted for neck, and work to end in patt, turn.

Rows 2–4: Ch 3, work in established wave patt. Fasten off.

Sleeves (Make 2)

Using larger hook and MC, ch 32 (32, 34, 36).

Row 1 (RS): Dc in 4th ch from hook and in each ch to end—30 (30 32, 34) dc, turn.

Row 2: Ch 3, working in fl, dc across, turn.

Row 3: Ch 3, working in bl, 1 dc in first st (1 st increased), dc across to last st, 2 dc in last st (1 st increased), turn—32 (32, 34, 36) dc.

Working in patt as est, cont to inc 1 dc at each edge of sleeve, every 3rd row another 10 (11, 12, 12) times—52 (54, 58, 60) dc.

Work even in dc until sleeve measures 17 (17, 17½, 17½)". Fasten off.

Finishing

With RS tog, sew shoulder seams. Place markers 8 (8½, 9, 9½)" on either side of shoulder seam. Matching center of sleeve to shoulder seams and edges to markers, sew in sleeves. Sew side and sleeve in one continuous seam.

Neck Edging

Rnd 1 (RS): Using MC and smaller hook, beg at shoulder seam, sc completely around neck, working sc3tog in each corner.

Rnd 2: Ch 1, sc in same st as joining, sc in each st around. Join and fasten off.

Sleeve Edging

With RS facing you and using larger hook and same color as for first wave, beg at seam and work 1 rnd of sc around lower sleeve. Join and fasten off.

Designer Tip

Use the three-quarter-length sleeves from the Luscious Limes Pullover on page 64 for a different look.

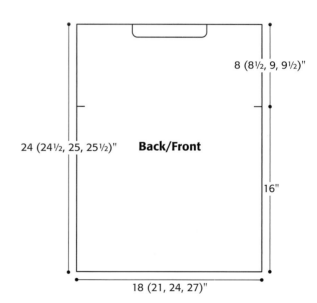

24 (24½, 25, 25½)" **Back/Front**

8 (8½, 9, 9½)"

16"

18 (21, 24, 27)"

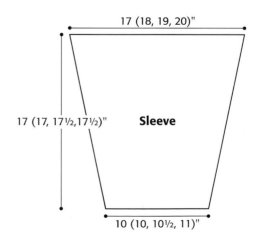

17 (18, 19, 20)"

17 (17, 17½,17½)" **Sleeve**

10 (10, 10½, 11)"

Positively Pink Girl's Jacket

What little girl wouldn't be thrilled with such a fancy jacket filled with so many pinks? She'll feel special wearing it, whatever the occasion.

Skill Level

Easy

Size

Children's 2 (4, 6)

Finished Measurements

Chest: 24 (27, 30)"

Length: 17½ (19½, 21½)"

Materials

- Approx 15 (17, 19) oz *total* of medium-weight yarns in mixed pinks or the colors of your choice, including some yarn that is fuzzy. Of this total amount, you will need approx 1 (1½, 2) oz of MC for sleeves and outer edging. (4)
- Size H-8 (5 mm) crochet hook or size required to obtain gauge
- Size G-6 (4 mm) crochet hook
- 3 pearl beads, 8" diameter
- Tapestry needle for sewing seams and weaving in ends

Gauge

6 sts and 5 rows = 2" using larger hook

Designer Tip

Individual stitches may be difficult to see when you are working with highly textured or fuzzy yarns. Place a marker on the first half double crochet stitch of every right side row to mark the transition from double crochet to half double crochet stitches and the shaping of the garment. The double crochet stitches cause the lower jacket (from armhole to bottom) to flare, while the half double crochet stitches keep the fit of the upper jacket closer to the body.

Body

Note: The body of the jacket is worked sideways, with double crochet stitches used for the lower body and half double crochet stitches used for the upper body. When the right side is facing you, the right edge is the bottom of the sweater and the left edge is the top of the sweater where the armhole and neck shaping will take place. Following the instructions, change colors at the end of every second row. Two rows of one color counts as one stripe. When changing colors, always pull the new color through the last loop worked with the old color.

Left Front

Using larger hook, ch 46 (50, 55).

Row 1 (RS): Dc in 4th ch from hook and in each of next 35 (39, 43) ch, 8 (9, 10) hdc, turn—44 (49, 54) sts.

Row 2: Ch 2 (counts as 1 hdc now and throughout), work 7 (8, 9) hdc, 36 (40, 44) dc. Change color, turn.

Row 3: Ch 3, work 35 (39, 43) dc, 8 (9, 10) hdc, turn.

Row 4: Ch 2, work 7 (8, 9) hdc, 36 (40, 44) dc. Change color, turn.

Rep rows 3 and 4 until 3 (3, 4) stripes are complete. End with WS row.

Shape Neck

With RS facing you and using color for next stripe, attach yarn to left edge of piece (neck) with sl st. Ch 8 (9, 10) and fasten off. Using same color as for ch added for neck, attach yarn to right edge of piece (bottom).

Left Shoulder

Row 1 (RS): Ch 3, work 35 (39, 43) dc, 16 (18, 20) hdc, turn—52 (58, 64) sts.

Row 2: Ch 2, work 15 (17, 19) hdc, 36 (40, 44) dc. Change color, turn.

Rep rows 1 and 2 until total of 7 (8, 9) stripes are complete. End with WS row.

With RS facing you and using color for next stripe, attach yarn to last hdc worked in last row (this is hdc next to dc section). Ch 16 (18, 20) for back and fasten off. Using same color as for ch added for neck, attach yarn to right edge of piece (bottom).

Left Armhole Opening

Row 1 (RS): Ch 3, work 35 (39, 43) dc, leave rem hdc from previous row unworked, work 1 hdc in each of next 16 (18, 20) ch, turn—52 (58, 64) sts.

Row 2: Ch 2, work 15 (17, 19) hdc, 36 (40, 44) dc, turn.

Back

Maintaining st placement of row 2, work total of 15 (17, 19) stripes for back. End with WS row. Fasten off.

With RS facing you and using color for next stripe, attach yarn to last hdc worked in last row (this is hdc next to dc section). Chain 16 (18, 20) for right armhole and fasten off. Using same color as for ch added for neck, attach yarn to right edge of piece (bottom).

Right Armhole Opening

Row 1 (RS): Ch 3, work 35 (39, 43) dc, leave rem hdc from previous row unworked, work 1 hdc in each of next 16 (18, 20) ch, turn—52 (58, 64) sts.

Row 2: Ch 2, work 15 (17, 19) hdc, 36 (40, 44) dc. Change color, turn.

Right Front and Shoulder

1 stripe complete. Maintaining st placement, work 3 more stripes. End with WS row.

Shape Neck

Row 1 (RS): Ch 3, work 35 (39, 43) dc, 8 (9, 10) hdc—44 (49, 54) sts. Leaving rem sts unworked, turn.

Row 2: Ch 2, work 7 (8, 9) hdc, 36 (40, 44) dc. Change color, turn.

1 stripe complete. Work 2 (2, 3) more stripes. Fasten off.

Sleeves (Make 2)

Using larger hook and MC, ch 25 (27, 29).

Row 1 (RS): Hdc in 3rd ch from hook and in each ch to end, turn—24 (26, 28) hdc.

Rows 2 and 3: Ch 2 (counts as 1 hdc now and throughout), hdc across, turn.

Row 4: Ch 2, 1 hdc in first st (1 st increased), hdc to last st, 2 hdc in last st (1 st increased), turn—26 (28, 30) hdc.

Row 5: Ch 2, hdc across, turn.

Cont to work in hdc, inc 1 st at each edge every 4th row another 4 (4, 5) times—34 (36, 40) hdc.

Work even until sleeve length measures 11 (12, 14)". Fasten off.

Flowers (Make 3)

Rnd 1: Using fuzzy yarn and smaller hook, ch 2, work 10 sc in 2nd ch from hook; join.

Rnd 2: *Ch 5 to form petal, sk 1 sc, sl st in next sc; rep from * another 4 times—5 petals. Sl st in first ch of beg ch 5. Fasten off.

Sew 1 pearl bead to center of each flower.

Finishing

With RS tog, sew shoulder seams. With RS tog, sew sleeve seams. Matching center of sleeve to shoulder seam and matching sleeve seam to underarm, sew in each sleeve.

Sleeve Cuffs

Rnd 1 (RS): Using fuzzy yarn or same yarn as sleeves and smaller hook, beg at seam, hdc around cuff, turn. Change to larger hook.

Rnds 2–6: Ch 2, hdc in each st; join.
Fasten off.

Outer Edging

Row 1 (RS): Using same yarn as for sleeves and smaller hook, beg at neck edge of left front, hdc down left front, across bottom, and up right front, making 3 hdc in each corner st, turn. Place markers on right front for 3 evenly spaced button loops. Change to larger hook.

Row 2: Ch 2, hdc to first marker for button loop, *ch 8, sl st in last hdc, hdc to next button loop; rep from * another 2 times, hdc to end and fasten off.

Sew flowers opposite button loops.

Collar

Row 1 (RS): Using same yarn as for sleeve cuffs and smaller hook, beg next to front edging of right front, work 16 (18, 20) sc to shoulder, 18 (20, 22) sc across back of neck, 16 (18, 20) sc to left front edging, turn—50 (56, 62) sc.

Row 2: Ch 1, work 1 sc in each st to end, turn. Change to larger hook.

Row 3: Ch 2, hdc to end, turn.

Rows 4–8: Ch 2, work 1 hdc in first st, hdc to last st, 2 hdc in last st, turn.
Fasten off.

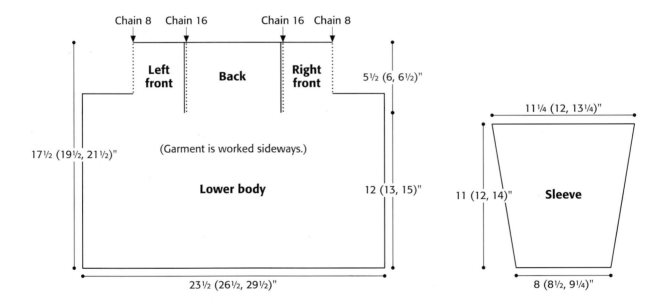

Girl's Pink Chapeau

For the crowning touch, this hat is a perfect complement to that special Positively Pink Girl's Jacket!

Skill Level
Easy

Size
One size fits children's 2, 4, and 6

Finished Measurement
20½" diameter

Materials

- MC: Approx 3 oz medium-weight fur yarn (4)
- CC1 and CC2: Approx 10 yds *each* of 2 coordinating medium-weight yarns (4)
- CC3: Approx 10 yds of fuzzy coordinating yarn for flower (4)
- Size H-8 (5 mm) crochet hook or size required to obtain gauge
- Size G-6 (4 mm) crochet hook
- Plastic marker
- 1 pearl bead, 8 mm diameter
- Tapestry needle for sewing seams and weaving in ends

Gauge

7 sts = 2" using larger hook

Hat

Note: This hat is worked in spiral rounds starting at the crown and working down toward the brim. Do not join the rounds unless the instructions specify. Place the plastic marker on the last stitch of each round, moving the marker as you complete each round.

Using larger hook and MC, ch 2.

Rnd 1: 8 sc in 2nd ch from hook.

Rnd 2: 2 sc in each st around—16 sc.

Rnd 3: *1 sc in first st, 2 sc in next st; rep from * around—24 sc.

Rnd 4: *1 sc in each of next 2 sts, 2 sc in next st: rep from * around—32 sc.

Rnd 5: *1 sc in each of next 3 sts, 2 sc in next st; rep from * around—40 sc.

Rnd 6: *1 sc in each of next 4 sts, 2 sc in next st; rep from * around—48 sc.

Rnds 7–14: Sc around. Tie in CC1 and join.

Rnd 15: Sc around. Tie in CC2 and join.

Brim

Rnd 16: *1 sc in first st, 2 sc in next st; rep from * around—72 sc.

Rnds 17–19: Sc around; join.
Fasten off.

Flower

Using smaller hook and CC3, ch 2.

Rnd 1: 5 sc in second ch from hook.

Rnd 2: Sl st in first sc of rnd 1, *ch 5, sl st in same st as joining, sl st in next st; rep from * around. Join and fasten off. Sew pearl bead to center of flower. Turn up brim and sew on flower.

Girl's Sassy Purse

Anyone knows that a lady doesn't leave home without her purse. Whether the purse is filled with makeup or a favorite fashion doll and clothes, it's a necessity. Use the bits and pieces of leftover yarns from the pink jacket to whip up this little accessory in no time. The jacket, purse, and hat make a just-right outfit for a day away from home.

Skill Level
Easy

Size
One size

Finished Measurements
7½" x 5½" (excluding handles)

Materials

- Approx 1½ oz *total* of medium-weight yarns in 12 different pinks or the colors of your choice, including some fuzzy yarn for flowers (**4**)
- Size H-8 (5 mm) crochet hook or size required to obtain gauge
- 2 pearl beads, 8 mm diameter
- 2 pink plastic purse handles
- Tapestry needle for sewing seams and weaving in ends

Gauge

6 hdc and 5 rows = 2"

Purse

Note: Change colors every other row as for Positively Pink Girl's Jacket on page 29. Two rows create one stripe.

Ch 23.

Row 1: Hdc in 3rd ch from hook and in each ch across, turn—22 hdc, turn.

Row 2: Ch 2 (counts as first hdc now and throughout), 1 hdc in each of next 21 sts. Change color, turn.

Rep row 2 until 12 stripes are complete. Fasten off.

Flower (Make 2)

Using fuzzy yarn, ch 2.

Rnd 1: 5 sc in 2nd ch from hook; join.

Rnd 2: *Ch 5, sl st in next sc; 1 petal made; rep from * 5 times; join. Fasten off.

Sew pearl bead to center of each flower.

Finishing

Fold purse in half. Sew sides, leaving 2" free at top on each side.

Find center point of front, fold ½" from each side to meet in center, forming pleat. Rep for back.

Sew flower to pleat on both front and back. Sew handles to purse.

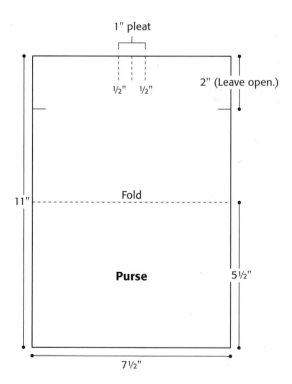

Ruffled Projects

Girl's Party-Purples Dress

Perfect for a party or summer outing for any little girl, this frilly dress with a pansy and ruffles would make a lovely Easter dress too.

Skill Level

Intermediate
■■■□

Size
Children's 2 (4, 6)

Finished Measurements
Chest: 27 (28, 29)"
Length: Approx 21¾ (25, 28¼)"

Materials

- Approx 7 (9, 11) oz *total* of fine-weight yarns in 3 shades of purple and white or the colors of your choice. Of this total amount, you will need approx 2 (2½, 3) oz of MC for bodice. **2**
- Size G-6 (4 mm) crochet hook or size required to obtain gauge
- Size F-5 (3.75 mm) crochet hook
- 8" length of green satin ribbon, ⅝" wide
- Sewing thread and needle
- Tapestry needle for sewing seams and weaving in ends
- 1 button, ½" diameter

Gauge

1 shell patt = 2" wide x 1¼" long using larger hook for skirt

7 hdc and 5 rows = 2" using larger hook for bodice

Skirt Back

Skirt is worked from waist to hemline.

With large hook and purple, ch 57 (65, 73).

Row 1 (RS): Sc in 2nd ch from hook, *sk 3 ch, (1 tr, ch 3, sl st in 3rd ch from hook; picot made) 6 times in next ch, 1 tr in same st; shell made; sk 3 ch, 1 sc in next ch; rep from * to end, turn—7 (8, 9) shells.

Row 2: Ch 5 (counts as 1 tr, plus ch 1); *sk 1 tr, FPdc around next dc, ch 1, sk 1 tr, FPsc around next tr, sk 1 tr, FPdc around next dc, sk last tr of shell, 1 tr in next sc; rep from * to end. Change color, turn.

Row 3: Ch 1; 1 sc in first st, *shell in FPsc behind center of previous shell, 1 sc in next single tr; rep from * to end, working last sc in 3rd ch of tch, turn.

Row 4: Ch 5 (counts as 1 tr, plus ch 1), turn; *sk 1 tr, FPdc around next tr, ch 1, sk 1 tr, ch 1, FPsc around next tr, ch 1, sk 1 tr, FPdc around next dc, ch 1, sk last tr of shell, 1 tr in next sc, ch 1; rep from * to end. Change color, turn.

Rep rows 3 and 4 until 10 (12, 14) ruffles are complete.

Rep row 3 once more—11 (13, 15) ruffles. Fasten off.

Bodice Back

With larger hook and MC, ch 49 (51, 53).

Row 1 (RS): Hdc in 3rd ch from hook and in each ch to end, turn—48 (50, 52) hdc.

Row 2: Ch 2, (counts as first hdc now and throughout); hdc to end, turn.

Work row 2 another 5 (5, 7) times. Fasten off.

Left Armhole

Row 1 (WS): Sk first 5 sts, attach yarn to next st. Ch 2 (counts as 1 hdc), 18 (19, 20) hdc, turn—19 (20, 21) sts.

Row 2: Ch 2, hdc to last 2 sts, hdc2tog, turn—18 (19, 20) hdc.

Row 3: Ch 1, beg hdc dec, hdc to end, turn—17 (18, 19) hdc.

Row 4: Ch 2; hdc to last 2 sts, hdc2tog, turn—16 (17, 18) hdc.

Row 5: Ch 2, hdc to end, turn.

Work row 5 another 3 (5, 7) times.

Left Neck

Row 1 (WS): Ch 2, hdc to last 6 sts, turn—10 (11, 12) hdc.

Row 2: Ch 1, beg hdc dec, hdc to end, turn—9 (10, 11) hdc.

Row 3: Ch 2; hdc to last 2 sts, hdc2tog, turn—8 (9, 10) hdc.

Work even in hdc until armhole measures 5 (5½, 6)". Fasten off.

Right Armhole

Row 1 (WS): Attach yarn to center st next to right back, ch 2, hdc in each st to last 5 sts, turn—19 (20, 21) hdc.

Row 2: Ch 1, beg hdc dec, hdc to end, turn—18 (19, 20) hdc.

Row 3: Ch 2; hdc to last 2 sts, hdc2tog, turn—17 (18, 19) hdc.

Row 4: Ch 1, beg hdc dec, hdc to end, turn—16 (17, 18) hdc.

Row 5: Ch 2, hdc to end, turn.

Work row 5 another 3 (5, 7) times.

Right Neck

Row 1 (WS): Sk first 6 sts, attach yarn to next st and ch 2 (counts as 1 hdc), hdc to end, turn—10 (11, 12) hdc.

Row 2: Ch 2, hdc to last 2 sts, hdc2tog, turn—9 (10, 11) hdc.

Row 3: Ch 1, turn, beg hdc dec, hdc to end, turn—8 (9, 10) hdc.

Work even in hdc until armhole measures 5 (5½, 6)". Fasten off.

Skirt Front

Work as for skirt back.

Bodice Front

Work as for bodice back to armholes. End with WS row. Fasten off.

Shape Armholes

Row 1 (WS): Sk first 5 sts, attach yarn to next st. Ch 2 (counts as 1 hdc), hdc to last 5 sts, turn—38 (40, 42) sts rem.

Rows 2–4: Ch 2, beg hdc, hdc to last 2 sts, hdc2tog, turn—32 (34, 36) hdc after row 4.

Work even until armholes measure 3½ (4, 4½)". End with WS row.

Left Neck

Row 1 (RS): Ch 2, 10 (11, 12) hdc, turn—10 (11, 12) hdc.

Row 2: Ch 1, beg hdc dec, hdc to end, turn—9 (10, 11) hdc.

Work rows 1 and 2 once more—8 (9, 10) hdc.

Work even in hdc until same length as back. Fasten off.

Right Neck

Row 1: Sk center 12 sts, attach yarn to next st. Ch 2, 10 (11, 12) hdc, turn—10 (11, 12) hdc.

Row 2: Ch 2, turn, hdc to last 2 sts, hdc2tog, turn—9 (10, 11) hdc.

Work rows 1 and 2 once more—8 (9, 10) hdc.

Work even in hdc until same length as back. Fasten off.

Finishing

With RS tog, sew shoulder seams. Sew side seams on bodice and skirt, taking care to leave all ruffles free on skirt. Whipstitch bodice to skirt, easing to fit.

Tie

Using larger hook and MC, make chain of approx 44 (46, 48)", sl st in 2nd ch from hook and in each ch to end. Fasten off. Weave tie in and out of first row of bodice at waist.

Armhole Edging

Using MC and smaller hook, beg at underarm seam, work 1 rnd sc around armhole. Join and fasten off. Rep for 2nd armhole.

Neck Edging

Using MC and smaller hook, beg at shoulder seam, work in sc around neckline, working 2 sc in corner back neck to left back corner (ch 3, sl st in last st made; button loop made), 2 sc in next st, sc to end. Join and fasten off. Sew on button.

Pansy

Use small amounts of 3 different purples.

Rnd 1: Using darkest purple, ch 2, work 10 sc in 2nd ch from hook, tie in and pull medium purple yarn through, cut dark purple; join.

Rnd 2: Ch 1 (1 hdc, 2 dc, 3 tr, 2 dc, 1 hdc; large petal made) all in same st as joining, sk next st, large petal in next st, tie in lightest shade, cut medium purple. *Sk 1 st, (9 hdc; small petal made) in next st; rep from * 3 times. Join to beg hdc. Change to darkest purple.

Rnd 3: *Sl st in next st, ch 2; rep from * around. Join and fasten off.

Cut ribbon in half and trim ends on the diagonal. Hand sew to back of flower for leaves. Placing flower at center neck front, tack in place.

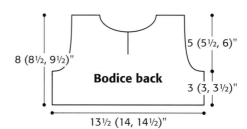

8 (8½, 9½)"
5 (5½, 6)"
Bodice back
3 (3, 3½)"
13½ (14, 14½)"

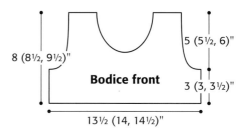

8 (8½, 9½)"
5 (5½, 6)"
Bodice front
3 (3, 3½)"
13½ (14, 14½)"

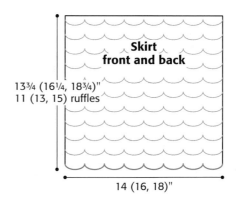

Skirt front and back
13¾ (16¼, 18¾)"
11 (13, 15) ruffles
14 (16, 18)"

Bead-Trimmed Bag

With its sassy, flirty ruffles, this little bag can have a completely different look with yarns of another color family or with different beads.

Skill Level
Intermediate
■■■□

Size
One size
Finished Measurements
Approx 9" x 7½"

Materials

- Approx 1½ oz *total* of medium-weight yarns in 7 shades of turquoise or the colors of your choice. Choose one color as the MC for the top and bottom of the bag. (4)
- Size H-8 (5 mm) crochet hook or size required to obtain gauge
- 72 silver beads, 6 mm diameter
- 2 silver beaded handles for bag
- 8½" x 10" piece of lining fabric
- Sewing needle and thread
- Tapestry needle for sewing seams and weaving in ends

Gauge

2 shells and 1 tier = 3"

Bag

The bag is worked from bottom to top. The yarn is cut when the instructions say to do so for threading beads. Ruffles are worked *without turning* work. You work from right to left on the first row, with each two double crochets creating one V-stitch. On the second row you work from left to right, and the shells are formed by working around each double crochet of the first row.

With MC, ch 75.

Row 1 (RS): Sk 7 chains. Make 2 dc in 8th ch from hook; V-st made; *ch 2, sk 2 ch, 1 dc in next ch, ch 2, sk 2 ch, V-st in next ch; rep from * end by skipping 2 ch and making 1 dc in last ch—12 V-sts, turn. Cut yarn, thread 12 beads onto yarn, and retie. Do not turn.

Row 2: *Working from left to right across row 1, turn work slightly and work (2 dc, 2 hdc, 2 sc) around post of nearest dc of first V-st, ch 1, slip bead close to hook, ch 1, rotate work slightly, now working around 2nd dc of same V-st from bottom to top of post, work (2 sc, 2 hdc, 2 dc), insert hook around post of next single dc and make 1 sc; rep from * to end, working last sc in 3rd ch of beg ch 8. Change color. Do not turn.

Row 3: Ch 5 (counts as 1 dc, plus ch 2), *V-st in ch 2 sp, ch 2, 1 dc in next single dc, ch 2; rep from * ending 1 dc in last st. Cut yarn and thread 12 beads on and retie. Do not turn.

Row 4: *Working from left to right across last row, turn work slightly and work (2 dc, 2 hdc, 2 sc) around post of nearest dc of first V-st, ch 1, slip bead close to hook, ch 1, rotate work slightly, now working around 2nd dc of same V-st from bottom to top of post, work (2 sc, 2 hdc, 2 dc), insert hook around post of next single dc and make 1 sc; rep from * to end, working last sc in 3rd ch of beg ch 8. Change color. Do not turn.

Work rows 2–4 another 5 times—7 shell tiers finished. Fasten off.

Bottom of Bag

Row 1 (RS): Working along beg ch of bag, attach MC to lower corner, ch 1, 1 sc in same st, *2 sc in ch 2 sp, 1 sc in center of shell, 2 sc in next ch 2 sp, 1 sc in next dc; rep from * to end.

Rows 2–4: Ch 1, sc in each st to end. Fasten off.

Assembly

Fold bag in half. Sew side seam, leaving shells free. Using MC, sl st across bottom of bag and fasten off.

Upper Bag Edging

With RS facing you and using same color as top row of shells, work 1 rnd of sc around top edge of bag. Join and fasten off.

Finishing

Lay bag on lining. Trace outline, adding ½" on all sides. Cut out lining. Fold lining fabric in half. With RS tog, sew ½" side seams. Insert into bag, turn down upper lining edge to fit just below top of bag. Using sewing needle and thread, slip-stitch lining to upper edge of bag. Sew on bag handles.

Glam Camisole

Two skeins of jazzy railroad-type ribbon, originally intended to be crocheted into Christmas scarves, can be just the touch to turn a simple camisole into something glamorous and special.

Skill Level

Easy

■■□□

Size

Small (Medium, Large, Extra Large)

Finished Measurements

Bust: 36 (40, 44, 48)"
Length: 16 (17, 18, 19)" (excluding ties)

Materials

- **MC:** Approx 4 (5, 6, 7) oz *total* of medium-weight railroad ribbon in variegated colors (4)
- **CC:** Approx 3 (4, 5, 6) oz of medium-weight yarn in a solid color (4)
- Size H-8 (5 mm) crochet hook or size required to obtain gauge
- Tapestry needle for sewing seams and weaving in ends

Gauge

5 shells = 8"

5 dc = 2"

Back

Note: Use MC (railroad ribbon) for all shell rows and for upper bodice.

Using MC, ch 70 (76, 82, 90).

Row 1: Dc in 7th ch from hook, *sk 2 ch, ch 2, 1 dc in next ch, sk 2 ch, ch 2 [(YO, insert hook in next ch, YO and draw yarn through 2 lps) twice, YO, pull yarn through 3 lps on hook; dc2tog made]; rep from * ending sk 2 ch, 1 dc in last ch. Cut MC and tie in CC.

Row 2: Ch 1, do not turn. 1 sc in dc, working from left to right, *work 5 FPdc (from top to bottom) around first post of dc2tog; half shell made, turn and work 5 FPdc (from bottom to top) around second post of same dc2tog; shell made; FPsc around next single dc, turn work to left and rep from * ending shell, 1 sc in 3rd ch of tch. Cut MC and tie in CC—11 (12, 13, 14) shells.

Row 3: Ch 3, *2 dc over ch 2 sp from row prior to shells, 1 dc in dc behind center of shell, 2 dc over next ch 2 sp, 1 dc in next dc; rep from * to end, turn—67 (73, 79, 87) dc.

Row 4: Ch 3, dc in each st to end, turn.

Row 5: Ch 5 (counts as dc, plus ch 2), sk 2nd and 3rd dc, *dc2tog in next st, ch 2, sk 2 sts, 1 dc in next st, ch 2; rep from * to end. Cut CC and tie in MC.

Work rows 2–5 another 2 times.

Next Row: Using CC, ch 3, *2 dc over ch 2 sp from row prior to shells, 1 dc in dc behind center of shell, 2 dc over next ch 2 sp, 1 dc in next dc; rep from * to end, turn.

Work another 5 rows even in dc. Piece should measure approx 8". Change to MC and work even in dc for another 3 (3½, 4, 4½)". Fasten off.

Shape Armholes and Bodice

Row 1 (RS): Sk first 6 (9, 10, 11) sts, attach MC to next st, ch 3 (counts as 1 dc), work in dc to last 6 (9, 10, 11) sts, turn—55 (55, 59, 65) dc.

Row 2: Dc3tog, dc to last 3 sts, dc3tog, turn—51 (51, 55, 61) dc.

Work row 2 another 6 (6, 7, 8) times—27 (27, 27, 29) dc rem. Fasten off.

Front

Work as for back to armhole shaping. End with WS row.

Shape Left Armhole and Bodice

Row 1: Skip first 6 (9, 10, 11) sts, attach ribbon to next st, ch 3 (counts as 1 dc), dc in each of next 21 (21, 25, 28) sts, dc3tog.

Row 2: Dc3tog, 1 dc in each of next 17 (17, 21, 24) sts, dc3tog, turn.

Row 3: Dc3tog, 1 dc in each of next 13 (13, 17, 20) sts, dc3tog, turn.

Row 4: Dc3tog, 1 dc in each of next 9 (9, 13, 16) sts, dc3tog, turn.

Row 5: Dc3tog, 1 dc in each of next 5 (5, 9, 12) sts, dc3tog, turn.

Sizes Small and Medium only:

Row 6 (WS): Dc3tog, 1 dc in next st, dc3tog, turn—3 sts rem.

Row 7: Dc3tog, fasten off.

Size Large only:

Row 6 (WS): Dc3tog, 1 dc in each of next 5 sts, dc3tog, turn—5 sts rem.

Row 7: Dc2tog, 1 dc in next st, dc2tog, turn—3 sts rem.

Row 8: Dc3tog, fasten off.

Size Extra Large only:

Row 6 (WS): Dc3tog, 1 dc in each of next 8 sts, dc3tog, turn—8 sts rem.

Row 7: Dc3tog, 1 dc in each of next 4 sts, dc3tog, turn—4 sts rem.

Row 8: (Dc2tog) twice, turn—2 sts rem.

Row 9: Dc2tog, fasten off.

Shape Right Armhole and Bodice

Row 1: Skip 1 st at center front, attach ribbon to next st, dc3tog, dc in each of next 22 (22, 26, 29) sts.

Beg with row 2, work as for left front.

Finishing

Make 1 tie at each upper front and each corner—4 ties total. Attach CC to corner and ch 46. Sl st in 2nd ch from hook and in each ch to end, sl st in beg st and fasten off.

Sew side seams.

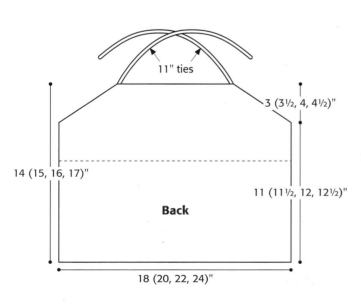

Back — 14 (15, 16, 17)"; 11" ties; 3 (3½, 4, 4½)"; 11 (11½, 12, 12½)"; 18 (20, 22, 24)"

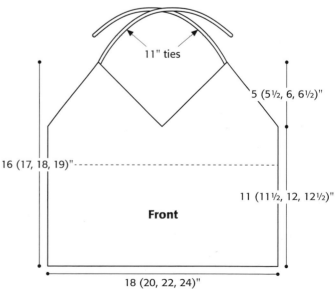

Front — 11" ties; 5 (5½, 6, 6½)"; 16 (17, 18, 19)"; 11 (11½, 12, 12½)"; 18 (20, 22, 24)"

Calypso Scarf

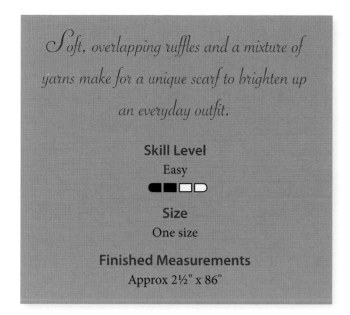

Soft, overlapping ruffles and a mixture of yarns make for a unique scarf to brighten up an everyday outfit.

Skill Level

Easy

Size

One size

Finished Measurements

Approx 2½" x 86"

Materials

- Approx 4 oz *total* of bulky-weight yarns in 3 shades of brown or the colors of your choice ⑤
- Size I-9 (5.5 mm) crochet hook or size required to obtain gauge
- Tapestry needle for sewing seams and weaving in ends

Gauge

5 dc = 2"

Scarf

Ch 197.

Row 1: Dc in 4th ch from hook, 1 dc in next ch, *(3 dc in next ch) 3 times, 1 dc in each of next 3 ch; rep from * to end, turn.

Row 2: Ch 4 (counts as 1 dc, plus ch 1 now and throughout), *1 dc in next dc, ch 1; rep from * to end, turn.

Row 3: Ch 4, *1 dc in next dc, ch 2; rep from * to end.

Fasten off.

Flower-Adorned V-neck Shell

An unusual combination of yarns creates a top for spring or summer. Or you can wear this top with velvet pants or a long skirt for a holiday occasion. Make it with a cotton yarn for a more casual look.

Skill Level

Easy

◧◼☐▭

Size

Small (Medium, Large, Extra Large)

Finished Measurements

Bust: 36 (40, 44, 48)"
Length: 18 (18½, 19, 19½)"

Materials

- **MC:** 4 (5, 6, 7) balls of Merino Frappe from Crystal Palace Yarns (80% merino, 20% nylon; 50 g; 140 yds) in color 290 White 〔4〕
- **CC1:** 2 (2, 3, 3) balls of Cotton Chenille from Crystal Palace Yarns (100% mercerized cotton; 50 g; 98 yds) in color 2342 Lime 〔4〕
- **CC2:** 2 (2, 3, 3) balls of Shimmer from Crystal Palace Yarns (86% acrylic, 14% nylon; 50 g; 90 yds) in color 9546 Tulips 〔4〕
- Size H-8 (5 mm) crochet hook or size required to obtain gauge
- Size E-4 (3.5 mm) crochet hook
- Size G-6 (4 mm) crochet hook
- Tapestry needle for sewing seams and weaving in ends

Gauge

6 sts and 7 rows = 2" using larger hook and MC

Back

First Ruffle

Using largest hook and CC1, ch 110 (122, 134, 146).

Row 1: Dc in 4th ch from hook and in each ch to end: 108 (120, 132, 144) dc, turn.

Row 2: Ch 3 (counts as first dc now and throughout), dc to end, turn.

Row 3: Beg dc2tog, *dc2tog; rep from * to end, turn—54 (60, 66, 72) dc. Change to MC.

Row 4: Ch 1, sc in each st to end, turn.

Rows 5 and 6: Ch 3, dc to end.
Fasten off.

Second Ruffle

Rows 1–3: Work as for rows 1–3 of first ruffle with MC, turn.

Holding first and second ruffles tog, with second ruffle overlapping first ruffle at back of work, and with WS facing you, still using MC, and working through both pieces, 1 sc in each st to end, turn.

Next 2 rows: Ch 3, dc to end.
Fasten off.

Third Ruffle

Rows 1–3: Work as for rows 1–3 of first ruffle with CC2, turn.

Holding second and third ruffles tog, with third ruffle overlapping second ruffle at back of work, WS facing you, still using CC2, and working through both pieces, 1 sc in each st to end. Fasten off.

Upper Bodice

Row 1 (RS): Using MC, ch 3, dc across top of 3rd ruffle to end.

Rep row 1 until back measures 10" from bottom of first ruffle. End after working WS row. Fasten off.

Shape Armhole

Row 1 (RS): Sk first 5 (6, 7, 9) sts, attach yarn to next st, ch 2, hdc in each st to last 5 (6, 7, 9) sts, turn—44 (48, 52, 54) sts.

Row 2: Beg hdc2tog, dc to last 2 sts, hdc2tog, turn—42 (46, 50, 52) sts.

Row 3: Ch 3, dc to end, turn.

Work rows 2 and 3 another 2 times—38 (42, 46, 48) hdc rem.

Left Shoulder

Rows 1–6 (WS): Ch 2; 1 hdc in each of next 9 (11, 12, 13) sts—10 (12, 13, 14) hdc.
Fasten off. Armhole depth should measure 8 (8½, 9, 9½)".

Right Shoulder

Row 1 (WS): Sk center 18 (18, 20, 20) back neck sts, attach yarn to next st, ch 2 (counts as 1 hdc), 9 (11, 12, 13) hdc, turn—10 (12, 13, 14) hdc.

Rows 2–6: Ch 2, hdc to end.
Fasten off. Armhole depth should measure 8 (8½, 9, 9½)".

Front

Work as for back to armhole shaping.

Left Shoulder and Neck

Row 1 (RS): Sk first 5 (6, 7, 9) sts, attach yarn to next st; ch 2 (counts as 1 hdc), 1 hdc in each of next 19 (21, 23, 24) sts, hdc2tog, turn—21 (23, 25, 26) sts.

Row 2: Beg hdc dec, hdc to end, turn—20 (22, 24, 25) sts.

Row 3: Beg hdc dec, hdc to last 2 sts, hdc2tog, turn—18 (20, 22, 23) sts.

Row 4: Beg hdc dec, hdc to end, turn—17 (19, 21, 22) sts.

Row 5: Beg hdc dec, hdc to last 2 sts, hdc2tog, turn—15 (17, 19, 20) sts.

Row 6: Beg hdc dec, hdc to end, turn—14 (16, 18, 19) sts.

Row 7: Beg hdc dec, hdc to last 2 sts, hdc2tog, turn—12 (14, 16, 17) sts.

Cont to dec 1 st, neck edge only another 2 (2, 3, 3) times every row—10 (12, 13, 14) sts rem for shoulder.

Work even until armhole depth measures 8 (8½, 9, 9½)".
Fasten off.

Right Shoulder and Neck

Row 1 (RS): Attach yarn to center st next to left front; ch 2 (counts as 1 hdc), hdc2tog, 1 hdc in each of next 19 (21, 23, 24) sts, leave rem 5 (6, 7, 9) sts unworked, turn—21 (23, 25, 26) sts.

Row 2: Ch 2, hdc to last 2 sts, hdc2tog, turn—20 (22, 24, 25) sts.

Row 3: Beg hdc dec, hdc to last 2 sts, hdc2tog, turn—18 (20, 22, 23) sts.

Row 4: Ch 2, hdc to last 2 sts, hdc2tog, turn—17 (19, 21, 22) sts.

Row 5: Beg hdc dec, hdc to last 2 sts, hdc2tog, turn—15 (17, 19, 20) sts.

Row 6: Ch 2, hdc to last 2 sts, hdc2tog, turn—14 (16, 18, 19) sts.

Row 7: Beg hdc dec, hdc to last 2 sts, hdc2tog, turn—12 (14, 16, 17) sts.

Cont to dec 1 st, neck edge only another 2 (2, 3, 3) times every row—10 (12, 13, 14) sts rem for shoulder.

Work even until armhole depth measures 8 (8½, 9, 9½)".
Fasten off.

Finishing

With RS tog, sew shoulder seams. Sew side seams, leaving ends of ruffles free. Sew ruffles tog individually at sides.

Armhole Edging

With RS facing you and using medium hook and MC, beg at underarm seam, sc around armhole. Join and fasten off. Rep on 2nd armhole.

Neck Edging

With RS facing you and using medium hook and MC, beg at shoulder seam, sc around neckline, working sc3tog at bottom of V-neck. Join and fasten off.

Large Flower (Make 1)

Using medium hook and CC2, ch 2.

Rnd 1: 9 sc in 2nd ch from hook.

Rnd 2: Sl st in fl of first sc, *ch 7, sl st in same fl, sl st in next sc; rep from * around.

Rnd 3: Sl st in bl of first sc, *ch 10, sl st in same bl, sl st in next sc; rep from * around. Join to beg sl st and fasten off.

Medium Lime Flower (Make 2)

Using smallest hook and CC1, ch 2. Sl st in first sc, *ch 5, sl st in same sc, sl st in next sc; rep from * around. Join to beg sc and fasten off.

Medium Lime Tendril (Make 2)

Using smallest hook and CC1, ch 10, 2 sc in 2nd ch from hook, 3 sc in each rem ch. Fasten off.

Medium White Flower (Make 4)

Using smallest hook and CC1, ch 2.

Rnd 1: 9 sc in 2nd ch from hook. Cut yarn and tie in MC.

Rnd 2: Sl st in first sc, *ch 7, sl st in same sc, sl st in next sc; rep from * around. Join and fasten off.

Medium Tulip Flower (Make 3)

Using smallest hook and CC2, ch 2.

Rnd 1: 7 sc in 2nd ch from hook.

Rnd 2: Sl st in fl of first sc, *ch 7, sl st in same sc, sl st in next sc; rep from * around.

Rnd 3: Sl st in bl of first sc, *ch 9, sl st in same sc, sl st in next bl; rep from * around. Join and fasten off.

Small Tulip Flower (Make 1)

Using smallest hook and CC2, ch 2.

Rnd 1: 5 sc in 2nd ch from hook.

Rnd 2: Sl st in fl of first sc, *ch 5, sl st in same sc, sl st in next sc; rep from * around.

Rnd 3: Sl st in bl of first sc, *ch 7, sl st in same sc, sl st in next bl; rep from * around. Join and fasten off.

Attach Flowers

Sew flowers across right shoulder and down left side of neckline as shown in photo.

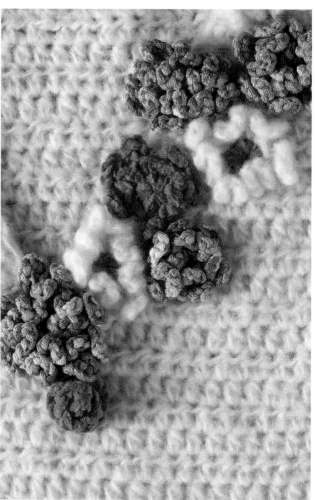

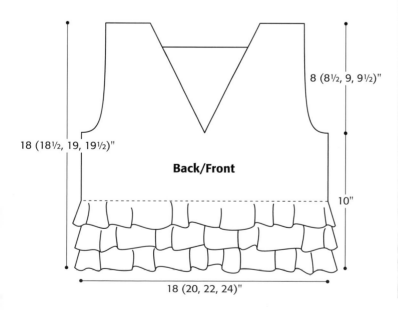

8 (8½, 9, 9½)"

18 (18½, 19, 19½)"

Back/Front

10"

18 (20, 22, 24)"

Cut-and-Tied Projects

Perky Peach V-neck Jacket

The longer length of this jacket is flattering to any body shape. Wear the jacket for any occasion, whether it's out for a walk, a shopping trip, or lunch with a friend.

Skill Level

Easy

■■□□

Size

Small (Medium, Large, 1X, 2X)

Finished Measurements

Bust: 38 (42, 46, 52, 56)"
Length: 24½ (25, 25½, 26, 26½)"

Materials

- Approx 25 (27, 29, 31, 33) oz *total* of medium-weight yarns in 20 different shades of peach or the colors of your choice (4)
- Size H-8 (5 mm) crochet hook or size required to obtain gauge
- Size G-6 (4 mm) crochet hook
- 10 wooden beads, 8 mm diameter
- Tapestry needle for sewing seams and weaving in ends

Gauge

6 sts and 7 rows = 2" using larger hook

Note: Change colors as desired using cut-and-tie techniques (see page 17).

Back

Using larger hook, ch 59 (65, 71, 79, 85).

Row 1 (RS): Hdc in 3rd ch from hook and in each ch to end, turn—58 (64, 70, 78, 84) hdc.

Row 2: Ch 2 (counts as first hdc now and throughout), hdc to end, turn.

Rep row 2 until piece measures 24½ (25, 25½, 26, 26½)". Fasten off.

Left Front

Using larger hook, ch 30 (33, 36, 40, 43).

Row 1 (RS): Hdc in 3rd ch from hook and in each ch to end—29 (32, 25, 39, 42) hdc, turn.

Row 2: Ch 2, hdc to end, turn.

Rep row 2 until piece measures 14". End with WS row.

Shape V-neck

Row 1 (RS): Ch 2, hdc to last 2 sts, hdc2tog, turn.

Row 2: Ch 2, hdc to end, turn.

Work rows 1 and 2 another 9 (9, 9, 11, 12) times—19 (22, 25, 27, 29) sts rem.

Work even until front is same length as back. Fasten off.

Right Front

Using larger hook, ch 30 (33, 36, 40, 43).

Row 1 (RS): Hdc in 3rd ch from hook and in each ch to end—29 (32, 25, 39, 42) hdc, turn.

Row 2: Ch 2, hdc to end, turn.

Rep row 2 until piece measures 14". End with WS row.

Shape V-neck

Row 1 (RS): Beg hdc2tog, hdc to end, turn.

Row 2: Ch 2, hdc to end, turn.

Work row 2 another 9 (9, 9, 11, 12) times—19 (22, 25, 27, 29) sts rem.

Work even until front is same length as back. Fasten off.

Sleeves (Make 2)

Using larger hook, ch 31 (33, 33, 35, 35).

Row 1 (RS): Hdc in 3rd ch from hook and in each ch to end, turn—30 (32, 32, 34, 34) hdc.

Row 2: Ch 2, hdc to end, turn.

Row 3: Ch 2, 1 hdc in first st (1 st increased), hdc to last st, 2 hdc in last st (1 st increased)—32 (34, 34, 36, 36) hdc, turn.

Cont to inc 1 st, each end of row, every other row another 10 (10, 12, 12, 14) times—52 (54, 58, 60, 64) hdc.

Work even until sleeve length measures 17 (17, 17½, 17½, 18)". Fasten off.

Finishing

With RS tog, sew shoulder seams. Place markers 8½ (9, 9½, 10, 10½)" on either side from shoulder seam for sleeve placement. Matching center of sleeve to shoulder seam and edges to markers, sew in sleeve. Sew side and sleeve in one continuous seam.

Sleeve Edging

With RS facing you and using smaller hook, beg at seam, work 1 rnd sc around lower sleeve. Join and fasten off.

Outer Edging

With RS facing you and using smaller hook, beg at side seam, work 2 rnds sc around outer edge, working 2 sc in each corner; join.

Ties

For each tie, cut a 3-yard length of the same yarn used for the edging, and thread on five beads. Folding the yarn in half, slide the middle bead to the center, make a knot approximately 1" above the bead, slide the next two beads to the knot just made, make a knot approximately 1" above the beads, slide the last two beads to the knot just made, and make a knot approximately 1" above the beads. Using the larger hook and holding both strands together, chain 20 and fasten off. Sew the ties to the wrong side of the front at the beginning of the V-neck shaping.

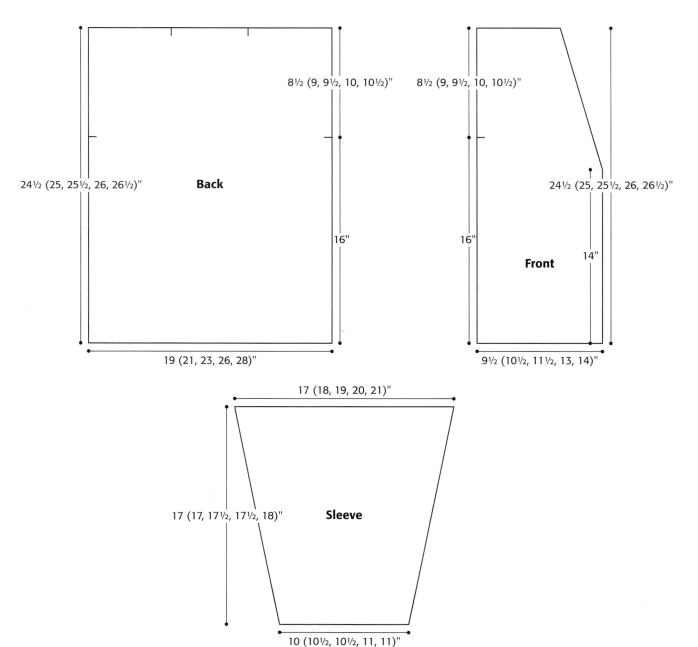

Shaped V-neck Jacket with Collar

Nipped in a bit at the waistline to flatter your figure, this jacket features a luxurious fur collar for an elegant touch. Wear it over a dress, with pants, or with a skirt to make an outfit really special.

Skill Level
Intermediate

Size
Small (Medium, Large, 1X, 2X)

Finished Measurements
Bust: 40 (44, 48, 52, 56)"
Length: 21 (21½, 22, 22½, 23)"

Materials

- Approx 28 (31, 34, 37, 41) oz *total* of medium-weight yarns in 24 shades of purple or the colors of your choice
- Size H-8 (5 mm) crochet hook or size required to obtain gauge
- Size G-6 (4 mm) crochet hook
- 2 jewelry pendants
- 1 yd of leather lacing
- Tapestry needle for sewing seams and weaving in ends

Gauge

6 sts and 7 rows = 2" using larger hook

Note: Change colors as desired using cut-and-tie techniques (see page 17).

Back

Using larger hook, ch 61 (67, 73, 79, 85).

Row 1 (RS): Hdc in 3rd ch from hook and in each ch to end—60 (66, 72, 78, 84) hdc, turn.

Rows 2 and 3: Ch 2 (counts as first hdc now and throughout), hdc to end, turn.

Shape Sides

Rows 4–6: Beg hdc2tog, work in hdc to last 2 sts, hdc2tog, turn—54 (60, 66, 72, 78) sts rem after row 6.

Rows 7–10: Ch 2, hdc to end, turn.

Rows 11–13: Ch 2, 1 hdc in first st (1 st increased), hdc to last st, 2 hdc in last st (1 st increased), turn—60 (66, 72, 78, 84) sts after row 13.

Work even in hdc until piece measures 12". End with WS row. Fasten off.

Shape Armholes

Row 1 (RS): Sk first 7 (8, 9, 10, 11) sts for armhole, attach yarn to next st, ch 2 (counts as first hdc), hdc across to last 7 (8, 8, 9, 11) sts—46 (50, 54, 58, 62) hdc, turn.

Work even until armhole depth measures 9 (9½, 10, 10½, 11)". Fasten off.

Left Front

Using larger hook, ch 31 (34, 37, 40, 43).

Row 1 (RS): Hdc in 3rd ch from hook and in each ch to end—30 (33, 36, 39, 42) hdc, turn.

Rows 2 and 3: Ch 2, hdc to end, turn.

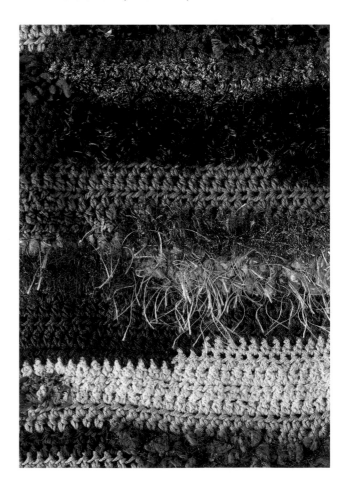

Row 4: Ch 2, work in hdc to last 2 sts, hdc2tog, turn—29 (32, 35, 38, 41) sts rem.

Row 5: Beg hdc2tog, work in hdc to end, turn—28 (31, 34, 37, 40) sts rem.

Row 6: Rep row 4—27 (30, 33, 36, 39) sts rem.

Rows 7–10: Ch 2, hdc to end, turn.

Row 11: Ch 2, 1 hdc in first st (1 st increased), hdc to end, turn—28 (31, 34, 37, 40) sts.

Row 12: Ch 2, hdc to last st, 2 hdc in last st (1 st increased), turn—29 (32, 35, 38, 41) sts.

Row 13: Rep row 11—30 (33, 36, 39, 42) sts.

Work even in hdc until piece measures 10". End with WS row.

Shape V-neck

Next row (RS): Hdc to last 2 sts, hdc2 tog (1 st decreased at neck edge).

Cont to dec 1 st at neck edge every other row another 9 times and AT SAME TIME, when length measures 12" end with WS row, fasten off, and beg armhole shaping as follows.

Shape Armhole

Next row (RS): Sk first 7 (8, 9, 10, 11) sts, attach yarn to next st, ch 2, hdc to last 2 sts, hdc2tog, turn.

After V-neck shaping, 13 (15, 17, 19, 21) hdc rem. Work even until armhole depth measures 9 (9½, 10, 10½, 11)". Fasten off.

Right Front

Using larger hook, ch 31 (34, 37, 40, 43).

Row 1 (RS): Hdc in 3rd ch from hook and in each ch to end—30 (33, 36, 39, 42) hdc, turn.

Rows 2 and 3: Ch 2, hdc to end.

Row 4: Beg hdc2tog, work in hdc to end, turn—29 (32, 35, 38, 41) sts rem.

Row 5: Ch 2, work in hdc to last 2 sts, hdc2tog, turn—28 (31, 34, 37, 40) sts rem.

Row 6: Rep row 4—27 (30, 33, 36, 39) sts rem.

Rows 7–10: Ch 2, hdc to end, turn.

Row 11: Ch 2, hdc to last st, 2 hdc in last st (1 st increased), turn—28 (31, 34, 37, 40) sts.

Row 12: Ch 2, 1 hdc in first st (1 st increased), hdc to end, turn—29 (32, 35, 38, 41) sts.

Row 13: Rep row 11—30 (33, 36, 39, 42) sts.

Work even in hdc until piece measures 10". End with WS row.

Shape V-neck

Next row (RS): Beg hdc2tog, hdc to end (1 st decreased at neck edge).

Cont to dec 1 st at neck edge every other row another 9 times and AT SAME TIME, when length measures 12" end with WS row. Beg armhole shaping as follows.

Shape Armhole

Next row (RS): Ch 2, beg hdc2tog, hdc to last 7 (8, 9, 10, 11) sts, turn.

Next row: Ch 2, hdc to end, turn.

After V-neck shaping, 13 (15, 17, 19, 21) hdc rem. Work even until armhole depth measures 9 (9½, 10, 10½, 11)". Fasten off.

Sleeves (Make 2)

Using larger hook, ch 29 (31, 31, 33, 35).

Row 1: Hdc in 3rd ch from hook and in each ch to end, turn—28 (30, 30, 32, 34) hdc.

Row 2: Ch 2, hdc to end, turn.

Row 3: Ch 2, 1 hdc in first st (1 st increased), hdc to last st, 2 hdc in last st (1 st increased), turn—30 (32, 32, 34, 36) hdc.

Row 4: Ch 2, hdc to end, turn.

Work rows 2–4 another 12 (13, 14, 15, 15) times—54 (58, 60, 64, 66) hdc.

Work even until sleeve measures 17 (17, 17½, 17½, 18)" Fasten off.

Finishing

With RS tog, sew shoulder seams. Place markers 9 (9½, 10, 10½, 11)" from shoulder seam on either side. Sew in sleeve. Sew side and sleeve in one continuous seam.

Cuff

Rnd 1 (RS): Beg at seam, using smaller hook, sc around lower sleeve; join.

Rnds 2–6: Ch 2, hdc around; join.
Fasten off.

Collar

Row 1 (RS): Beg at V-neck shaping, using smaller hook, work 38 sc to shoulder seam, 2 sc in next st, (8 [8, 8, 10, 10] sc, sc2tog, 8 [8, 8, 10, 10] sc) across back neck to shoulder seam, 2 sc in next st, 38 sc from shoulder seam to V-neck shaping, turn—97 (97, 97, 101, 101) sc.

Row 2: Ch 2, 1 hdc in first st, hdc around collar to last st, 2 hdc in last st, turn—99 (99, 99, 103, 103) hdc.

Rows 3–6: Rep row 2—107 (107, 107, 111, 111) sts after row 6. Fasten off.

Cut leather lacing in half. Knot one pendant to each tie. Knot each tie to front.

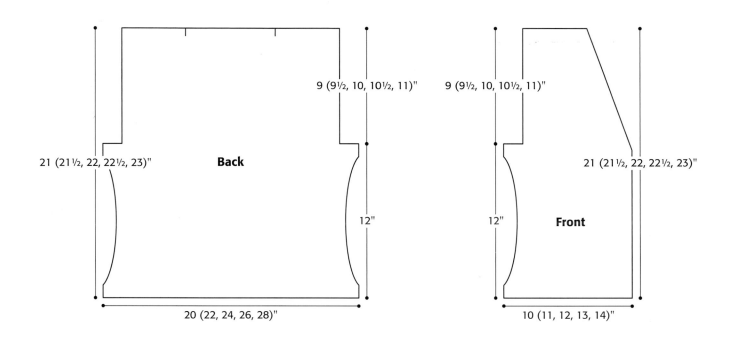

9 (9½, 10, 10½, 11)"

9 (9½, 10, 10½, 11)"

21 (21½, 22, 22½, 23)"

Back

12"

21 (21½, 22, 22½, 23)"

12"

Front

20 (22, 24, 26, 28)"

10 (11, 12, 13, 14)"

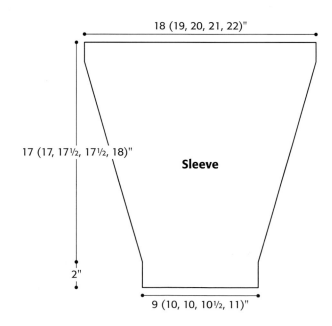

18 (19, 20, 21, 22)"

17 (17, 17½, 17½, 18)"

Sleeve

2"

9 (10, 10, 10½, 11)"

Pink Ruffled-Edge Cropped Jacket

This jacket is so feminine in pink. Make several versions for yourself and as gifts for friends who appreciate the latest styles.

Skill Level
Easy

Size
Small (Medium, Large, Extra Large)

Finished Measurements
Bust: 36 (40, 44, 48)"
Length: 13½ (14, 14½, 15)"

Materials

- Approx 17 (19, 21, 23) oz *total* of medium-weight yarns in 17 shades of pink or the colors of your choice. Of this total amount, you will need approx 6 (7, 8, 9) oz in one color for edging.
- Size H-8 (5 mm) crochet hook or size required to obtain gauge
- Size G-6 (4 mm) crochet hook
- Tapestry needle for sewing seams and weaving in ends

Gauge

6 sts and 7 rows = 2" using larger hook

Note: Change colors as desired using cut-and-tie techniques (see page 17).

Back

Using larger hook, ch 55 (61, 67, 73).

Row 1: Hdc in 3rd ch from hook and in each ch to end—54 (60, 66, 72) hdc, turn.

Row 2: Ch 2 (counts as first hdc now and throughout), hdc in each hdc to end, turn.

Rep row 2 until back measures 13½ (14, 14½, 15)". Fasten off.

Right Front

Using larger hook, ch 28 (31, 34, 37).

Row 1: Hdc in 3rd ch from hook and in each ch to end—27 (30, 33, 36) hdc, turn.

Row 2: Ch 2, hdc to end, turn.

Rep row 2 until piece measures 5". End with WS row.

Shape Neck

Row 1 (RS): Beg hdc2tog, hdc to end—26 (29, 32, 35) hdc, turn.

Row 2: Ch 2, hdc to end, turn.

Work rows 1 and 2 another 8 (9, 10, 11) times (dec 1 st at neck edge every other row)—18 (20, 22, 24) hdc rem for shoulder.

Work even in hdc until front is the same length as back. Fasten off.

Left Front

Using larger hook, ch 28 (31, 34, 37).

Row 1: Hdc in 3rd ch from hook and in each ch to end—27 (30, 33, 36) hdc, turn.

Row 2: Ch 2, hdc to end, turn.

Rep row 2 until piece measures 5". End with WS row.

Shape Neck

Row 1 (RS): Ch 2, hdc to last 2 sts, hdc2tog—26 (29, 32, 35) hdc, turn.

Row 2: Ch 2, hdc to end, turn.

Work rows 1 and 2 another 8 (9, 10, 11) times (dec 1 st at each edge every other row)—18 (20, 22, 24) hdc rem for shoulder.

Work even in hdc until front is same length as back. Fasten off.

Sleeves (Make 2)

Using larger hook, ch 29 (31, 33, 35).

Row 1: Hdc in 3rd ch from hook and in each ch to end—28 (30, 32, 34) hdc, turn.

Rows 2 and 3: Ch 2, hdc to end, turn.

Row 4: Ch 2, 1 hdc in first st (1 st increased), hdc to last st, 2 hdc in last st (1 st increased)—30 (32, 34, 36) hdc, turn.

Rep rows 2–4, inc 1 st at each edge of sleeve, every 3rd row another 11 (11, 12, 12) times—52 (54, 58, 60) hdc.

Work even in hdc until sleeve measures 16 (16, 16½, 16½)". Fasten off.

Finishing

With RS tog, sew shoulder seams. Place markers 8½ (9, 9½, 10)" from shoulder seam on either side. Matching center of sleeve to shoulder seam, sew in sleeve. Sew sleeve and side in one continuous seam.

Front Edging

Rnd 1 (RS): Using yarn set aside for edging and smaller hook, sc around outer edges of jacket, working 3 sc in each corner and at beg of V-neck shaping for each front; join.

Rnd 2: Ch 3, 2 dc in same st as joining, *3 dc in next st; rep from * around; join.
Fasten off.

Sleeve Edging

Rnd 1 (RS): Using same yarn as used for front edging, beg at seam, sc around sleeve; join.

Rnd 2: Ch 3, 2 dc in same st as joining, *3 dc in next st; rep from * around. Join and fasten off.

Rnds 3 and 4: Ch 3, 1 dc in each st around; join. Fasten off.

Rep on 2nd sleeve.

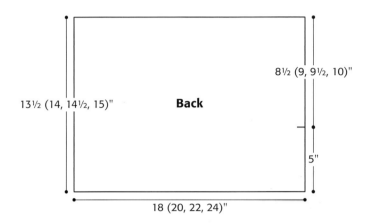

Back
13½ (14, 14½, 15)"
8½ (9, 9½, 10)"
5"
18 (20, 22, 24)"

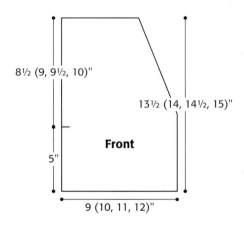

Front
8½ (9, 9½, 10)"
13½ (14, 14½, 15)"
5"
9 (10, 11, 12)"

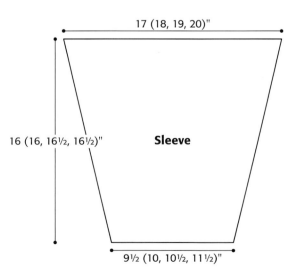

Sleeve
17 (18, 19, 20)"
16 (16, 16½, 16½)"
9½ (10, 10½, 11½)"

Luscious Limes Pullover

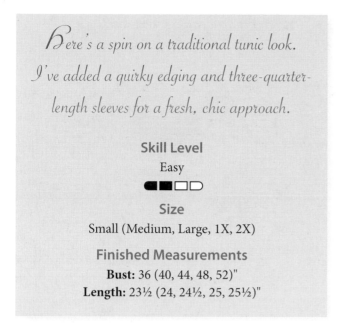

Here's a spin on a traditional tunic look. I've added a quirky edging and three-quarter-length sleeves for a fresh, chic approach.

Skill Level
Easy

■■□□

Size
Small (Medium, Large, 1X, 2X)

Finished Measurements
Bust: 36 (40, 44, 48, 52)"
Length: 23½ (24, 24½, 25, 25½)"

Materials

- 21 (23, 25, 27, 29) oz *total* of medium-weight yarns in 23 different shades of lime and green or the colors of your choice (4)
- Size H-8 (5 mm) crochet hook or size required to obtain gauge
- Size G-6 (4 mm) crochet hook
- Tapestry needle for sewing seams and weaving in ends

Gauge

6 hdc and 7 rows = 2" using larger hook

Note: Change colors as desired using cut-and-tie techniques (see page 17).

Back

Using larger hook, ch 55 (61, 67, 73, 79).

Row 1 (RS): Hdc in 3rd ch from hook and in each ch to end, turn—54 (60, 66, 72, 78) hdc.

Row 2: Ch 2 (counts as first hdc now and throughout), hdc in each st to end, turn.

Rep row 2 until back measures 23½ (24, 24½, 25, 25½)". Fasten off.

Front

Work as for back until front measures 15". End with WS row.

Divide for Left Front

Row 1 (RS): Ch 2, 26 (29, 32, 35, 38) hdc, turn—27 (30, 33, 36, 39) sts. This row creates neck opening.

Work even until neck opening measures 5½ (6, 6½, 7, 7½)". End with WS row.

Shape Left Neck

Row 1 (RS): Ch 2, hdc to last 6 (7, 8, 9, 9), hdc2tog, turn—21 (23, 25, 27, 30) sts.

Row 2: Ch 2, hdc to end, turn.

Row 3: Ch 2, hdc to last 2 sts, hdc2tog, turn—20 (22, 24, 26, 29) sts.

Work rows 2 and 3 another 3 times—17 (19, 21, 23, 26) sts rem for shoulder.

Work even until piece measures same length as back. Fasten off.

Right Front

Row 1 (RS): Attach yarn to center st next to left front, ch 2 (counts as 1 hdc), hdc to end of row—27 (30, 33, 36, 39) hdc, turn.

Work even over same sts until neck opening measures 5½ (6, 6½, 7, 7½)". End with WS row. Fasten off.

Shape Right Neck

Row 1 (RS): Sk first 5 (6, 7, 8, 8) sts, attach yarn to next st, beg hdc2tog, hdc to end, turn—21 (23, 25, 27, 30) sts.

Row 2: Ch 2, hdc to end of row, turn.

Row 3: Ch 2, beg hdc dec, hdc to end, turn—20 (22, 24, 26, 29) sts.

Work rows 2 and 3 another 3 times—17 (19, 21, 23, 26) sts rem for shoulder.

Work even until piece measures same length as back. Fasten off.

Sleeves (Make 2)

Using larger hook, ch 37 (39, 39, 41, 43).

Row 1: Hdc in 3rd ch from hook and in each ch to end—36 (38, 38, 40, 42) hdc, turn.

Row 2: Ch 2, 1 hdc in first st (1 st increased), hdc to last st, 2 hdc in last st (1 st increased)—38 (40, 40, 42, 44) hdc, turn.

Row 3: Ch 2, hdc to end, turn.

Rep rows 2 and 3, inc 2 sts every other row another 7 (7, 9, 9, 10) times—52 (54, 58, 60, 64) hdc.

Work even in hdc until sleeve length measures 12 (12, 12½, 12½, 13)". Fasten off.

Finishing

With RS tog, sew shoulder seams. Place markers 8½ (9, 9½, 10, 10½)" on either side of shoulder seam. Matching center of sleeve to shoulder seam, sew in sleeve. Sew sleeve and side in one continuous seam.

Neck Edging

With RS facing you and using smaller hook, work sc around neck opening. Join and fasten off.

Sleeve Edging

Rnd 1 (RS): Using same yarn as used for neck edging and smaller hook, beg at seam, sc around sleeve; join.

Rnd 2: Ch 1, 1 sc in same st as joining, 1 sc in each of next 2 sts, *ch 5, sk 1 sc, sl st in 3rd sc to right, inserting hook in loop just made, work 9 sc in same loop, 1 sc in each of next 3 sc of rnd 1; rep from * around, adjusting sts if necessary. Join and fasten off.

Lower Edging

Work as for sleeve edging.

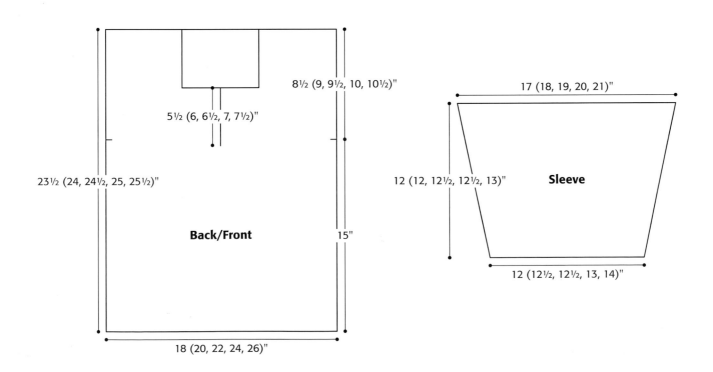

8½ (9, 9½, 10, 10½)"

5½ (6, 6½, 7, 7½)"

23½ (24, 24½, 25, 25½)"

Back/Front   15"

18 (20, 22, 24, 26)"

17 (18, 19, 20, 21)"

12 (12, 12½, 12½, 13)"   **Sleeve**

12 (12½, 12½, 13, 14)"

This classic crewneck pullover is anything but ordinary. In a shorter, updated length and chock-full of color and texture, it's sure to become a wardrobe staple to be worn on many an occasion.

Skill Level

Intermediate

■■■□

Size

Small (Medium, Large, 1X, 2X)

Finished Measurements

Bust: 38 (42, 46, 50, 54)"

Length: 20½ (21, 21½, 22, 22½)"

Materials

- Approx 18 (20, 22, 24, 26) oz *total* of medium-weight and bulky-weight yarns in 20 shades of turquoise or the colors of your choice
- Size G-6 (4 mm) crochet hook or size required to obtain gauge
- Size H-5 (5 mm) crochet hook or size required to obtain gauge
- Size E-4 (3.5 mm) crochet hook
- Tapestry needle for sewing seams and weaving in ends

Gauge

6 sts and 7 rows = 2" using largest hook and medium-weight yarn or using medium hook and bulky-weight yarn

Note: Change colors as desired using cut-and-tie techniques (see page 17).

Back

Using largest hook and medium-weight yarn, ch 59 (65, 71, 77, 83).

Row 1 (RS): Hdc in 3rd ch from hook and in each ch to end, turn—58 (64, 70, 76, 82) hdc.

Row 2: Ch 2 (counts as first hdc now and throughout), hdc to end, turn.

Rep row 2 until piece measures 10" for all sizes. End with WS row. Fasten off.

Shape Armhole

Row 1 (RS): Sk first 5 (6, 7, 9, 11) sts, attach yarn to next st, ch 2 (counts as 1 hdc), hdc to last 5 (6, 7, 9, 11) sts, turn—48 (52, 56, 58, 60) hdc.

Row 2: Ch 2, hdc to end, turn.

Row 3: Beg 2hdctog, hdc to last 2 sts, hdc2tog, turn—46 (50, 54, 56, 58) hdc.

Work rows 2 and 3 another 2 times—42 (46, 50, 52, 54) hdc.

Work even in hdc until armhole depth measures 8½ (9, 9½, 10, 10½)". Fasten off.

Front

Work as for back until armhole depth measures 5 (5½, 6, 6½, 7)". End with WS row.

Shape Left Neck

Row 1 (RS): Ch 2, 14 (16, 17, 18, 19) hdc, turn—15 (17, 18, 19, 20) hdc.

Row 2: Beg hdc2tog, hdc to end, turn—14 (16, 17, 18, 19) hdc rem.

Row 3: Ch 2, hdc to end.

Work rows 2 and 3 another 3 times—11 (13, 14, 15 16) hdc rem for shoulder.

Work even until armhole depth measures 8½ (9, 9½, 10, 10½)". Fasten off.

Shape Right Neck

Row 1 (RS): Sk center 12 (12, 14, 14, 14) sts for neck, attach yarn to next st, ch 2 (counts as 1 hdc), hdc to end, turn—15 (17, 18, 19, 20) hdc.

Row 2: Ch 2, hdc to last 2 sts, hdc2tog, turn—14 (16, 17, 18, 19) hdc.

Row 3: Ch 2, hdc to end, turn.

Work rows 2 and 3 another 3 times—11 (13, 14, 15, 16) hdc rem for shoulder.

Work even until armhole depth measures 8½ (9, 9½, 10, 10½)". Fasten off.

Sleeves (Make 2)

Using largest hook, ch 35 (37, 39, 41, 43).

Row 1: Hdc in 3rd ch from hook and in each ch to end, turn—34 (36, 38, 40, 44) hdc.

Rows 2–5: Ch 2, hdc to end, turn.

Row 6: Ch 2, 1 hdc in first st (1 st increased), hdc to last st, 2 hdc in last st (1 st increased), turn—32 (34, 36, 38, 42) hdc.

Cont to work in hdc, inc 1 st at each edge of sleeve every 6 rows another 5 times—46 (48, 50, 52, 54) hdc.

Work even until sleeve length measures 14 (14, 14½, 14½, 15)". End with WS row. Fasten off.

Sleeve Cap

Row 1 (RS): Sk first 5 (5, 7, 9, 11) sts, attach yarn to next st, ch 2 (counts as 1 hdc), hdc to last 5 (6, 7, 9, 11) sts, turn—36 (36, 36, 34, 32) hdc.

Size Small only:

Row 2 (WS): Ch 2, hdc to end, turn.

Row 3: Beg hdc dec, hdc across to last 2 sts, hdc2tog, turn—34 hdc.

Row 4: Hdc to end, turn.

Rows 5–14: Work rows 3 and 4 another 5 times—24 hdc at end of row 12.

Row 15: Beg hdc dec, hdc across to last 2 sts, hdc2tog, turn—22 hdc.

Rows 16–18: Beg hdc3tog, hdc across to last 3 sts, hdc3tog—10 sts rem at end of row 17.
Fasten off.

Size Medium only:

Row 2 (WS): Ch 2, hdc to end, turn.

Row 3: Beg hdc dec, hdc across to last 2 sts, hdc2tog, turn—34 hdc.

Row 4: Ch 2, hdc to end, turn.

Rows 5–16: Work rows 3 and 4 another 6 times, turn—22 hdc at end of row 15.

Rows 17–19: Beg hdc3tog, hdc across to last 3 sts, hdc3tog—10 sts rem at end of row 19.
Fasten off.

Size Large only:

Row 2 (WS): Ch 2, hdc to end, turn.

Row 3: Beg hdc2tog, hdc across to last 2 sts, hdc2tog, turn—34 hdc.

Row 4: Ch 2, hdc to end, turn.

Rows 5–17: Work rows 2 and 3 another 6 times—22 hdc at end of row 17.

Rows 18–20: Beg hdc3tog, hdc across to last 3 sts, hdc3tog, turn—10 sts rem at end of row 20.
Fasten off.

Size 1X only:

Row 2 (WS): Ch 2, hdc to end, turn.

Row 3: Beg hdc2tog, hdc across to last 2 sts, hdc2tog, turn—32 hdc.

Row 4: Ch 2, hdc to end, turn.

Rows 5–18: Work rows 3 and 4 another 7 times—18 sts rem at end of row 17.

Row 19: Ch 2, hdc to end, turn.

Rows 20 and 21: Beg hdc3tog, hdc across to last 3 sts, hdc3tog—10 sts rem at end of row 21.
Fasten off.

Size 2X only:

Row 2 (WS): Ch 2, hdc to end, turn.

Row 3: Beg hdc2tog, hdc across to last 2 sts, hdc2tog, turn—30 hdc.

Rows 4 and 5: Ch 2, hdc to end, turn.

Rows 6–17: Work rows 2–4 another 4 times—22 sts rem at end of row 14.

Rows 18–20: Beg hdc2tog, hdc to last 2 sts, hdc2tog, turn—16 sts rem at end of row 19.

Row 21: Beg hdc3tog, hdc to last 3 sts, hdc3tog—12 sts rem. Fasten off.

Finishing

With right sides together, sew the shoulder seams. Sew in the sleeves. Sew the side and sleeve in one continuous seam.

Sleeve Cuff Edging

Row 1 (RS): Using smallest hook, working in free loops of beg ch, attach yarn in end st at seam, ch 15; sc in 2nd ch from hook and in each of next 13 ch—14 sc. Sl st in each of next 2 ch, turn.

Row 2: Do not chain. Sk 2 sl sts, sc in bl of each of next 14 sc, turn.

Row 3: Ch 1, turn; sc in bl of 14 sc, sl st in next 2 ch, turn.

Rep rows 2 and 3 to end. Sew cuff seam.

Lower Edging

Row 1 (RS): Using smallest hook, working in free loops of beg ch, attach yarn in end st at side seam, ch 11; sc in 2nd ch from hook and in each of next 9 ch—10 sc. Sl st in each of next 2 ch, turn.

Row 2: Do not chain. Sk 2 sl sts, sc in bl of each of next 10 sc, turn.

Row 3: Ch 1, sc in bl of 10 sc, sl st in next 2 ch, turn.

Rep rows 2 and 3 to end. Sew edging seam.

Neck Edging

Rnd 1: Using smallest hook, beg at side seam, sc around neck; join.

Rnd 2: Ch 4, sc in 2nd ch from hook and in each of next 2 st from rnd 1, 3 sc, sl st in each of next 2 sts, turn.

Row 3: Sk both sl sts, sc in bl of each of next 2 sc, turn.

Row 4: Ch 1, sc in bl of each of next 3 sc, sl st in next 2 sts from rnd 1, turn.

Rep rows 3 and 4 around neck. Fasten off, leaving tail. Thread tail in tapestry needle and sew ribbing ends tog on WS.

Beg at shoulder seam, using medium hook, sc around neckline. Join and fasten off.

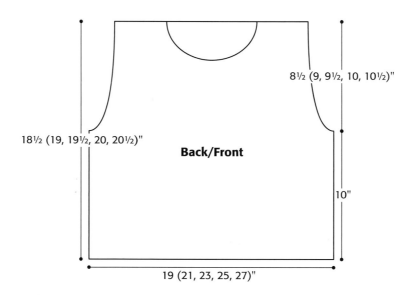

8½ (9, 9½, 10, 10½)"

18½ (19, 19½, 20, 20½)"

Back/Front

10"

19 (21, 23, 25, 27)"

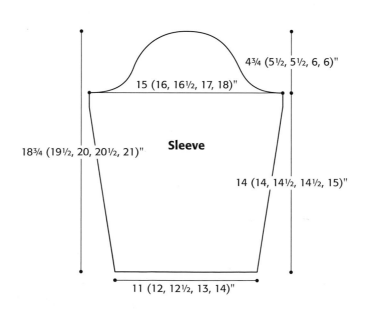

4¾ (5½, 5½, 6, 6)"

15 (16, 16½, 17, 18)"

18¾ (19½, 20, 20½, 21)"

Sleeve

14 (14, 14½, 14½, 15)"

11 (12, 12½, 13, 14)"

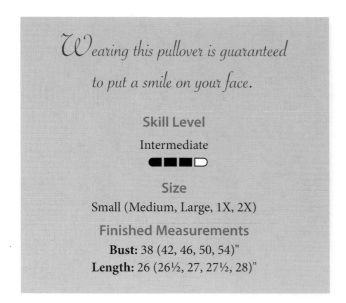

Wearing this pullover is guaranteed to put a smile on your face.

Skill Level

Intermediate

◼◼◼◻

Size

Small (Medium, Large, 1X, 2X)

Finished Measurements

Bust: 38 (42, 46, 50, 54)"

Length: 26 (26½, 27, 27½, 28)"

Materials

- Approx 19 (21, 23, 25, 27) oz *total* of medium-weight and bulky-weight yarns in 22 different shades of red or the colors of your choice ④ ⑤
- Size G-6 (4 mm) crochet hook or size required to obtain gauge
- Size H-8 (5 mm) crochet hook or size required to obtain gauge
- Size E-4 (3.5 mm) crochet hook
- Tapestry needle for sewing seams and weaving in ends

Gauge

6 sts and 7 rows = 2" using largest hook and medium-weight yarn and using medium hook and bulky-weight yarn

Note: Change colors as desired using cut-and-tie techniques (see page 17).

Back

Using largest hook and medium-weight yarn, ch 59 (65, 71, 77, 83).

Row 1: Hdc in 3rd ch from hook and in each ch to end, turn—58 (64, 70, 76, 82) hdc.

Row 2: Ch 2 (counts as first hdc now and throughout), hdc to end.

Rep row 2 until piece measures 25 (25½, 26, 26½, 27)". Fasten off.

Front

Work as for back until piece measures 17". End with WS row.

Shape Left Neck

Row 1 (RS): Ch 2, work 26 (29, 32, 25, 38) hdc, hdc2tog, turn—28 (31, 34, 37, 40) hdc.

Row 2: Ch 2, hdc to end.

Cont to dec 1 st at neck edge every other row another 9 (9, 10, 10, 11) times—19 (22, 24, 27, 29) sts rem for shoulder.

Work even in hdc until neck length measures 9 (9½, 10, 10½, 11)". Fasten off.

Shape Right Neck

Row 1 (RS): Attach yarn at center next to left neck, beg hdc dec, hdc to end, turn—28 (31, 34, 37, 40) hdc.

Row 2: Ch 2, hdc to end, turn.

Cont to dec 1 st at neck edge every other row another 9 (9, 10, 10, 11) times—19 (22, 24, 27, 29) sts rem for shoulder.

Work even in hdc until neck length measures 9 (9½, 10, 10½, 11)". Fasten off.

Sleeves (Make 2)

Using largest hook and medium-weight yarn, ch 33 (35, 35, 37, 37).

Row 1: Hdc in 3rd ch from hook and in each ch to end, turn—32 (34, 34, 36, 36) hdc.

Row 2: Ch 2, hdc to end, turn.

Row 3: Ch 2, 1 hdc in first st (1 st increased), hdc to last st, 2 hdc in last st (1 st increased)—34 (36, 36, 38, 38) hdc.

Sizes Small, Medium, and Large only:

Cont to inc 1 st at each end of row every 3rd row another 10 (11, 12) times—54 (58, 60) hdc.

Work even until piece measures 17 (17, 17½)". Fasten off.

Sizes 1X and 2X only:

Cont to inc 1 st at each end of row every other row another 13 (14) times—64 (66) hdc.

Work even until piece measures 17½ (18)". Fasten off.

Finishing

With RS tog, sew shoulder seams. Place markers 9 (9½, 10, 10½, 11)" on either side of side seam. Sew in sleeves, matching center of sleeve to seam and edges to markers.

Sleeve Edging

Row 1 (RS): Using smallest hook, working in free loops of beg ch, attach yarn in end st at side seam, ch 7, sc in 2nd ch from hook and in each of next 5 ch—6 sc, sl st into each of next 2 sts, turn.

Row 2: Sk 2 sl sts, sc in bl of each of next 5 sc, turn.

Row 3: Ch 1, sc in bl of each of next 5 sc, sl st in each of next 2 sts, turn.

Rep rows 2 and 3 to end. Fasten off.

Sew side and sleeve in one continuous seam.

Neck Edging

Using medium hook, beg at shoulder seam, work 1 rnd sc around neck. Join and fasten off.

Lower Edging

Rnd 1 (RS): Using largest hook, beg at seam, 1 sc in each st around; join.

Rnd 2: Ch 7, dc in 4th ch from hook, 1 dc in same st as joining, *sk 3 sts, 1 dc in next st, ch 4, 1 dc in 4th ch from hook, 1 dc in same st as last dc; rep from * around. Join to 3rd ch of beg ch 7. Fasten off. Sew edging seam.

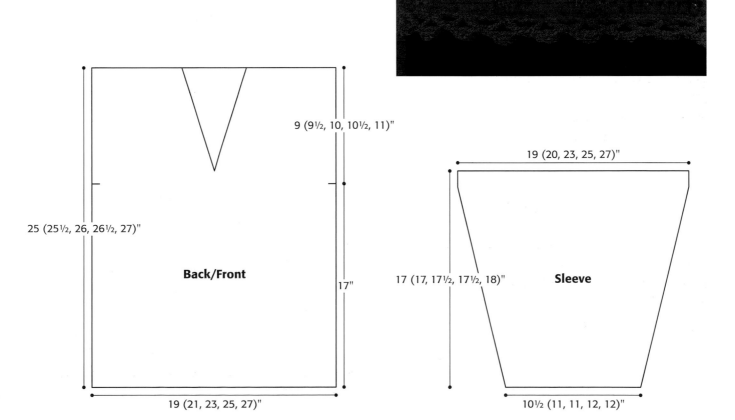

9 (9½, 10, 10½, 11)"

25 (25½, 26, 26½, 27)"

Back/Front

17"

19 (21, 23, 25, 27)"

19 (20, 23, 25, 27)"

17 (17, 17½, 17½, 18)"

Sleeve

10½ (11, 11, 12, 12)"

Romantic Cocoon Jacket

Straight from the latest fashion scene, this jacket will surprise you by how quickly it works up.

Skill Level
Easy

Size
Small (Medium, Large, 1X, 2X)

Finished Measurements
Bust: 36 (40, 44, 48, 52)"
Back length: 13 (13½, 14, 14½, 15)"

Materials

- Approx 8 (10, 12, 14, 16) oz *total* of medium-weight yarns in 19 shades of blue or the colors of your choice for bodice and sleeves (4)
- Approx 6 (8, 10, 12, 14) oz of medium-weight yarn in MC for collar and outer edge (4)
- Size H-8 (5 mm) crochet hook or size required to obtain gauge
- Size G-6 (4 mm) crochet hook
- 1 bead, any size
- 1 locking jewelry clasp
- Tapestry needle for sewing seams and weaving in ends

Gauge

6 hdc and 5 rows = 2" using larger hook

Body

Note: The back is worked first in the cut-and-tie technique from the bottom up, and then the fronts are attached to the back at the shoulders and worked from the top down. The outer edge and collar are worked in the main color circularly around the outer perimeter of the body in one piece. The sleeves are worked separately in the cut-and-tie technique and sewn in.

Back

Using larger hook and medium-weight yarn, ch 55 (61, 67, 73, 79).

Row 1 (RS): Hdc in 3rd ch from hook and in each ch to end, turn—54 (60, 66, 78, 78) hdc.

Row 2: Ch 2 (counts as first hdc now and throughout), hdc to end, turn.

Rep row 2 until piece measures 8 (8½, 9, 9½, 10)". End with WS row.

Left Front

Row 1 (RS): Ch 2, hdc in each of next 16 (19, 21, 24, 26) hdc, turn—17 (20, 22, 25, 27) sts.

Rows 2–5: Ch 2, hdc to end, turn.

Row 6 (WS): Beg hdc2tog, hdc to end, turn—16 (19, 21, 24, 26) hdc.

Row 7: Ch 2, hdc to last 2 sts, hdc2tog, turn—15 (18, 20, 23, 25) hdc.

Work rows 6 and 7 another 3 times—9 (12, 14, 17, 19) hdc.

Work even until left front measures 8 (8½, 9, 9½, 10)" from shoulder (row 1 of left front). Fasten off.

Right Front

Row 1 (RS): Sk center 20 (20, 22, 22, 24) sts, attach yarn to next st, ch 2 , hdc in each of next 16 (19, 21, 24, 26) hdc, turn—17 (20, 22, 25, 27) hdc.

Rows 2–5: Ch 2, hdc to end, turn.

Row 6 (WS): Ch 2, hdc to last 2 sts, hdc2tog, turn—16 (19, 21, 24, 26) hdc.

Row 7: Beg hdc2tog, hdc to end, turn—15 (18, 20, 23, 25) hdc.

Work rows 6 and 7 another 3 times—9 (12, 14, 17, 19) hdc.

Work even until right front measures 8 (8½, 9, 9½, 10)" from shoulder (row 1 of right front). Fasten off.

Outer Edge and Collar

Note: The outer edge and collar are worked in the round in the main color. Follow the instructions carefully. After the first round, each round is joined and then turned as if worked in rows.

Rnd 1: Using MC, fold in half at shoulders so bottom edges of fronts and back align. With RS facing you, work 54 (60, 66, 72, 78) sc across bottom of back, work 9 (12, 14, 17, 19) sc across bottom of front, work 26 (31, 32, 34, 36) sc from bottom of front opening to shoulder, work 20 (20, 22, 22, 24) sc across back neck, work 26 (31, 32, 34, 36) sc from shoulder to lower front, work 9 (12, 14, 17, 19) sc along second front, join with sl st to first st of rnd—124 (146, 158, 174, 188) sc.

Rnd 2: Ch 3 (counts as 1 dc), 1 dc in same st as joining, *sk 2 sts, (2 dc, ch 1, 2 dc—shell made) in next st; rep from * ending (2 dc, ch 1) in beg st of rnd—last shell made, turn.

Rnds 3–5: Rep rnd 2, turning work every rnd.

Rnd 6: Ch 3, 2 dc in same st as joining, *(3 dc, ch 1, 3 dc—shell made) in ch 1 sp of next shell; rep from * ending (3 dc, ch 1) in beg st of rnd, turn.

Rnds 7–10: Sl st in ch 1 just made, 2 dc in same st as joining, *(3 dc, ch 1, 3 dc—shell made) in ch 1 sp of next shell, rep from * ending (3 dc, ch 1) in beg ch 1 sp. Fasten off.

Sleeves (Make 2)

Using larger hook, ch 29 (31, 33, 35, 37).

Row 1 (RS): Hdc in 3rd ch from hook and in each ch to end, turn—28 (30, 32, 34, 36) hdc.

Row 2: Ch 2, hdc to end, turn.

Row 3: Ch 2, 1 hdc in first st (1 st increased), 1 hdc in each st to last st, 2 hdc in last st (1 st increased), turn—30 (32, 34, 36, 38) hdc.

Cont to work in hdc, inc 1 st at each edge every 3rd row another 11 (11, 12, 12, 13) times—52 (54, 58, 60, 64) hdc.

Work even until sleeve length measures 17 (17, 17½, 17½, 18)". Fasten off.

Flower

Rnd 1: Using smaller hook and a light shade of blue, ch 2. Work 7 sc in 2nd ch from hook; join.

Rnd 2: 2 sc in each st around—14 sc. Tie in dark blue; join *(1 sc, 1 dc, 1 tr, 1 dc, 1 sc—petal made) in fl of next st, sl st in next st; rep from * around—7 petals made. Change to a light blue fuzzy yarn; join.

Rnd 3: Sl st in bl of next st and working behind petals of rnd 2, ch 3 (counts as 1 dc), 4 dtr in same bl, *sl st in next bl, 5 dtr in next bl; rep from * around, sl st in last bl. Join and fasten off.

Finishing

With RS tog, sew sleeve seams. Sew in sleeves. Sew bead to center of flower. Sew locking jewelry clasp to center back of flower.

Sleeve Edging

With RS facing you and using smaller hook, beg at seam, work sc around lower sleeve edge. Join and fasten off.

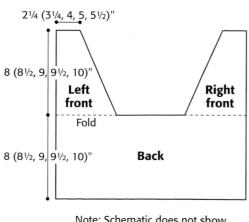
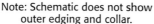

Note: Schematic does not show outer edging and collar.

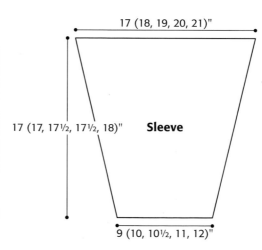

Capelet

Materials

- **MC:** 4 balls of Merino Frappe from Crystal Palace Yarns (80% merino, 20% nylon; 50 g; 140 yds) in color 122 Olallie (4)
- **CC1:** 1 ball of Shimmer from Crystal Palace Yarns (86% acrylic, 14% nylon; 50 g; 90 yds) in color 2845 Grape (4)
- **CC2:** 1 ball of Shimmer from Crystal Palace Yarns (86% acrylic, 14% nylon; 50 g; 90 yds) in color 4639 Ocean Blue (4)
- **CC3:** 2 balls of Party Ribbon from Crystal Palace Yarns (100% nylon; 50 g; 87 yds) in color 402 Ultra Blues (3)
- Size I-9 (5.5 mm) crochet hook or size required to obtain gauge
- Size H-8 (5 mm) crochet hook
- Plastic stitch markers
- Tapestry needle for sewing seams and weaving in ends

Gauge

5 dc = 2" using larger hook and MC

Capelet

Note: Change colors as instructed.

Beg at back neck, using larger hook and CC2, ch 10.

Row 1: Dc in 4th ch from hook and in each ch to end, turn—8 dc.

Row 2: Ch 3 (counts as 1 dc now and throughout), 1 dc in sp between first 2 sts, *2 dc in sp between next 2 sts; rep from * to end, turn—14 dc.

Row 3: Ch 3, 1 dc in sp between first 2 sts, *1 dc in sp between next 2 sts, 2 dc in sp between next 2 sts; rep from * across, turn—20 dc.

Row 4: Ch 3, 1 dc in sp between first 2 sts, place marker between last 2 sts, *(1 dc in sp between next 2 sts) twice, 2 dc in sp between next 2 sts, place marker between last 2 sts; rep from * another 4 times, (1 dc in sp between next 2 sts) twice, 2 dc in sp between last 2 sts, place marker between last 2 sts, turn—26 dc. Change to cut-and-tie technique using all four colors.

Row 5: Ch 3, 1 dc in sp between first 2 sts, *1 dc in sp between next 2 sts, rep from * to marker, 2 dc in marked sp, slip marker between last 2 sts just made; rep from first * to end—32 dc.

Rows 6–20: Cont to work in same manner as previous rows, which creates inc of 6 sts per row, working these rows. At end of row 20, cut yarn and tie in MC—122 dc.

Rows 21–29: Ch 3, cont to work as previous rows, working with MC only. Do not cut yarn, turn—176 dc.

Row 30: Ch 1, sc in first and each st across row; cut yarn and tie in CC3.

Ruffle Edging

Row 31: Ch 1, 1 sc in first st, *ch 7, 1 sc in next st; rep from * to end of row. Fasten off.

Front-Opening Edging

Row 1: Tie in MC, using smaller hook, still using MC, work sc around front opening.

Row 2: Turn to work along row 30, using smaller hook, 1 sc in first st, *ch 7, 1 sc in next st; rep from * to end. Fasten off.

Ties (Make 2)

Using smaller hook and CC3, attach yarn to lower front, make chain 15" long. Sc in 2nd ch from hook and in each ch to end, sl st in same st as beg. Fasten off.

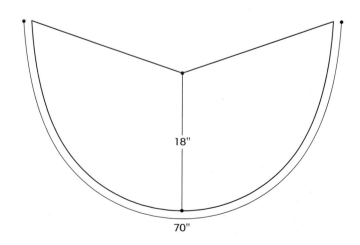

18"

70"

Twister Scarf

*J*ust the thing to perk up a plain top or outfit, this narrow scarf can also be worn over a jacket or coat. If you prefer a looser, unstructured look, instead of coiling the finished scarf, allow it to fall into folds naturally.

Skill Level

Easy

Size

One size

Finished Measurements

Approx 2½" x 66"

Materials

- Approx 5 oz *total* of medium-weight yarns in 19 shades of pink and red or the colors of your choice
- Size H-8 (5 mm) crochet hook or size required to obtain gauge
- Tapestry needle for sewing seams and weaving in ends

Gauge

7 sts and 5 rows = 2"

Note: Change colors as desired using cut-and-tie techniques (see page 17).

Scarf

Make chain approx 60" long.

Row 1: 2 dc in 4th ch from hook, *3 dc in next ch; rep from * to end, turn.

Rows 2 and 3. Ch 3 (counts as 1 dc now and throughout), 1 dc in each st to end. Fasten off at end of row 3.

Twist scarf into corkscrew shape.

About the Author

When her daughters began to complain that their closets and drawers
were overflowing with hand-crocheted and knitted sweaters, Darla turned
her passion into a profession as a designer in 1978. With more than 2,500
published designs, she continues to develop and create designs to her heart's
content for national publishers and yarn companies.

Acknowledgments

Many thanks to Martingale & Company for allowing me to bring my dream of *Creative Crochet* to fruition. In
particular, I want to thank Donna Druchunas, my technical editor, not only for the great job she has done but
especially for being such a dream to work with. She made the process as easy as possible, and I appreciate her
so much!

It's such a pleasure for me to share these techniques with you crocheters. Much heartfelt appreciation is
extended to Susan Druding, owner of Crystal Palace Yarns, with whom I've worked for two decades. She
generously contributed the highest-quality yarns in stunning colors for three projects in this book, which
enabled me to share different looks and ideas with you.